Published 2017 by Mary Jane Walker

A Maverick Traveller Ltd.

PO BOX 44 146, Point Chevalier, Auckland 1246

www.a-maverick.com

ISBN-13: 978-1542534505

ISBN-10: 154253450X

Some names have been changed to disguise and protect certain individuals and to help protect against defamation. All events are true and are an accurate record, subject to the disclaimer below.

Disclaimer

The author has recalled events, places and conversations from her memories of them. Although the author and publisher have made every effort to ensure that the information in this book was correct at the time of publication, the author and publisher do not assume and hereby disclaim any liability to any party for any loss, damage, or disruption caused by errors or omissions, whether such errors or omissions result from negligence, accident,or any other cause.

Notes on Image Sources

Maps not credited in the text have been sourced from the *US Central Intelligence Agency World Factbook*. All other maps and aerial views are credited with the original source. Caption credit abbreviations for maps, photographs and aerial views are as follows:

DOC: New Zealand Department of Conservation.

AJT: this refers to l'Association Jonque-Tion 79, a French association set up in 1979 to build and operate the junk La Dame de Canton / Elf-Chine.

All photographs in the book are property of Mary Jane Walker unless otherwise credited.

Contents

Mary Jane Walker is a New Zealand-based maverick and author, born with a wanderlust gene.

Mary Jane has spent two years naked on a Chinese Junk; got so lost she ended up in Robin Hood's hiding-place; drunk hallucinogenic tea in the Amazon rainforest; and kicked a nuclear-powered submarine.

She has travelled much of the world and has incredible stories to share about her adventures. There is more to travelling than boutique restaurants and fancy hotels.

She has walked to Mount Everest Base Camp and seen the work and life of Sherpas. Danced and prayed in many churches, temples and mosques. Traversed various parts of the Camino de Europa. Explored the stunning landscapes of New Zealand. Visited remote parts of the Arctic while pulled by a team of dogs. And all while meeting amazing people along the way.

The urge to explore is not just something that's in us: for some people it's really in us. So, for a richer travelling experience, not just about countries but their people and histories as well, read on.

Facebook: facebook.com/amavericktraveller
Instagram: @a_maverick_traveller
Twitter: @Mavericktravel0
Email: maryjanewalker@a-maverick.com
Linkedin: Mary Jane Walker

www.**a-maverick**.com

Other books by Mary Jane Walker

A Maverick New Zealand Way

Discover the stunning back country of New Zealand. Come along with Mary Jane on over fifty walks and mountain ascents throughout the islands of New Zealand. Offering an interesting account of New Zealand history alongside tales of modern-day adventure, it is the perfect read to inspire you to get outdoors in New Zealand.

http://a-maverick.com/books/new-zealand-way

A Maverick Cuban Way   *Release: 8 August 2017*

Trek with Mary Jane to Fidel's revolutionary hideout in the Sierra Maestra. See where the world nearly ended and the Bay of Pigs and have coffee looking at the American Guantánamo Base, all the while doing a salsa to the Buena Vista Social Club. Go to where Columbus first landed but don't expect to have wifi on your phone, only in hotspots using a card. People are proud and there's one doctor for every 150 people. Mary Jane loved it and did it.

http://a-maverick.com/books/cuban-way

A Maverick Pilgrim Way   *Release: 22 August 2017*

Follow the winding ancient roads of pilgrims across the continent of Europe. The Camino de Europa traverses nations, mountains and ranges. Mary Jane has dedicated her life to completing it, one section at a time.

http://a-maverick.com/books/pilgrim-way

A Maverick USA Way   *Release: 5 September 2017*

Mary Jane took AMTRAK trains to East Glacier, West Glacier, Tetons, Estes and Yosemite national parks before the snow hit. She loved the Smithsonian museums and after seeing a live dance at the Native Museum, she decided to go to Standing Rock. It was a protest over land rights and drinking water, at 30 below zero! She loved Detroit which is going back to being a park, and Galveston and Birmingham, Alabama. She was there during the election and was not surprised Trump won. She was tired of being mistaken for being a homeless person because she had a back pack and left San Francisco because of it.

http://a-maverick.com/books/USA-way

A Maverick Himalayan Way   *Release: 16 September 2017*

Mary Jane walked for ninety days and nights throughout the Himalayan region and Nepal, a part of the world loaded with adventures and discoveries of culture, the people, their religions and the beautiful landscapes. She visited the Hindu Kush in Pakistan and listened to the Dalai Lama in Sikkim, India. It is a journey of old and new. So, come trekking in the Himalayas with Mary Jane.

http://a-maverick.com/books/himalayan-way

A Maverick Inuit Way and the Vikings   *Release: 1 October 2017*

Mary Jane's adventures in the Arctic take her dog sledding in Greenland, exploring glaciers and icebergs in Iceland, and meeting some interesting locals. She found herself stuck on a ship in the freezing Arctic Ocean amongst icebergs, and had her car windows almost blown out by gale force winds! Take a ride through the Arctic and its fascinating history.

http://a-maverick.com/books/inuit-way

Plus: *A Maverick Australian Way*, due out on 16 October 2017

Introduction

I'M a maverick. Always have been, and always will be. In the last three decades of international travel, I've spent two years naked on a Chinese junk; got so lost I ended up in Robin Hood's hiding place; drank hallucinogenic tea in the Amazon rainforest; and kicked a nuclear-powered submarine. That's just a fraction of the adventures that I have had.

I have travelled the world, from the Arctic Circle to volunteering for the New Zealand Department of Conservation on an uninhabited island.

The urge to explore is not just something that's in our minds. For some people it's really in us, deep within us. If you're crazy about cultures, new experiences, maps, exploring and finding the road less travelled, you're not alone. You're just like me.

Embrace your inner gypsy. By giving in to the urge to travel you are on a one-way path to contentment.

And so, to my story.

It begins with what I still think of as a defining point in my life: a voyage from Phuket to Gabon on a Chinese junk built at the instigation of one very determined young man, Niels Lutyens...

CHAPTER ONE
Not all Junk is Junk

As a child, Niels had been obsessed with Chinese junks: the traditional-looking sailing ships that have been around since the early 2nd Century AD. There had been a miniature replica of one on the table in his room in Paris. He had planned to build one since he turned twenty. I remember him often looking at the miniature replica when I visited him later on.

Niels' maternal grandfather had been the French ambassador to the United States. Perhaps that had something to do with the fact that the French Government eventually sponsored the building of a junk at the Chinese Naval Dockyard in Guangzhou in1979, with Niels on the organising committee: *l'Association Jonque-Tion 79*. Nobody had built a traditional Chinese junk for over thirty years, and finding skilled labourers in what was essentially a lost art took some time. But eventually, in 1981, it was completed.

La Dame De Canton (The Lady of Canton) was twenty-five metres long, made of teak with cotton sails, bamboo battens and three masts, which in nautical parlance are the foremast, the mainmast, and the mizzen (rear or stern) mast. The boat was huge, in other words. And unfortunately, not entirely waterproof either: it used to leak periodically, and the deck let in the rain. The mainmast broke once and the mizzenmast broke twice in rough seas throughout the voyage. There was a motor and a mechanic, and we were grateful to make use of both in emergencies.

In 1981, the French state oil company *Société Nationale Elf- Aquitaine* — the word Elf was short for *Essence et Lubrifiants de France*, that is,

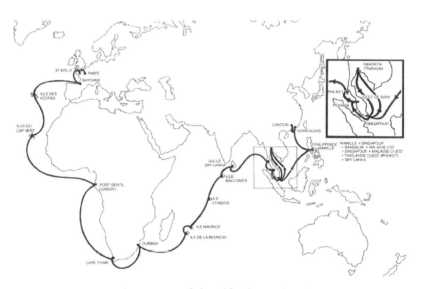

The Voyage of the Elf-Chine *(AJT)*

French Gasoline and Lubricants — sponsored a journey of more than thirty thousand kilometres from Guangzhou to Paris, provided the boat was renamed *Elf-Chine*, that is to say, Elf-China.

Along the way, the *Elf-Chine* as it now was, would become the first Chinese Junk ever to round the Cape of Good Hope. The junk would later be renamed *La Dame de Canton* after passing through one other name, and is now tied up on the River Seine in Paris as a floating restaurant, under its original name.

When we joined the junk in Phuket, in spite of all this sponsorship, the crew were out of money and were living off rice. Maree and I gave them a

The Elf-Chine, *a. k. a.* La Dame de Canton *(AJT)*

donation of $180 and that paid for fresh fruit and vegetables for two weeks.

We sailed to many places around South East Asia and beyond on *Elf-Chine*; a whole host of wild ocean adventures.

We partied in port. Several among the crew including Niels were musicians, so they'd sing Edith Piaf and play the grand piano, drums, saxophone and guitar until four in the morning. We'd make our own super-strong sake, the traditional Japanese wine, and the crew would smoke lots of marijuana. I preferred to smoke Indonesian clove cigarettes, very aromatic and enjoyable, without side effects.

We were baked and naked on a junk, far from oppressive societal rules.

Our first trip on the boat was to Sri Lanka, which in those days was an island filled with backpacker hostels. It wasn't the international tourist hotel hotspot it is now. The trip was supposed to take two and a half weeks through the Andaman Sea and the Bay of Bengal. It took just over a month.

For the most part the sea was calm and everybody pitched in smoothly with three-hour shifts cooking, cleaning, and manning the boat.

The crew on deck would vary between six and twenty-two people. When there were only six people on deck there was more room to move. *Elf-Chine* was so big that it required a minimum crew of four on deck at any time, even in good weather, and six when things turned bad. The junk didn't have a steering wheel, just a three metre long tiller (helm) which needed two people to handle it. In bad weather nobody got any rest; when a storm hit it became exhausting and dangerous. Even when the boat was full we were busy, but it meant that we were covered when the sky crashed into the ocean, so to speak — or if someone accidentally set the boat on fire while cooking dinner.

For the kitchen was tiny and cooking for so many people on a large six-ringed gas burner took some getting used to. Every time the boat swayed, the kitchen did as well. And everything on the burners slid off. During a storm it was impossible. But people still needed to eat to keep their strength up, so I persevered.

One night, about halfway through the trip, a violent thunderstorm hit. It was so intense I didn't think the boat would make it through. The cotton sails were ripping in the wind, but we weren't able to fix them until the weather cleared. We were pretty much stranded in the middle of the ocean, in a storm, in a boat that leaked. Torrential rain is battering the crew on deck, the sails are billowing and breaking and I'm trying to cook something to feed twenty people. At least I was protected from the elements, but the kitchen felt like it was attached to a rollercoaster. It was intense.

While I was cooking there was a heave and the boat lurched to the side. The handwritten recipe slid onto the burner, caught fire, flew across the room and instantly attached itself to the teak wall, which must have soaked up too much grease because it erupted in flames. Fortunately, just as this happened, a crew-member arrived at the door to grab a drink and was able to help me beat down the flames. The storm was bad enough; adding a fire at sea to the mix was more than enough excitement for one night.

Eventually the storm passed. We fixed the sails, which always resulted in bloody fingers because of how you had to hold and stitch them, and we continued on our way.

Boat life was tough. Money was constantly an issue and Chinese junks weren't made to sail too far from land. They're not ocean-going vessels so they get beaten up in deep water. Living conditions were cramped and no-one spoke English. After a while I learnt how to speak French fluently, which made a huge difference to how I was treated by the all-French crew.

But there were upsides, the parties of course, the enjoyment of sailing when the weather was good, and an endless abundance of fish. Whenever we were bored we'd put a line out and catch fish or sharks, which the crew would kill with an axe. It reminded me of when my mum used to work in a fish and chip shop in Hawkes Bay. She'd batter and fry up shark — it was good fresh eating.

We also had a dog on-board called Jules, a beautiful Labrador. But sadly she died a month into the trip after eating rat bait, shortly after we got to Sri Lanka.

Fresh eggs were a-plenty: chickens roaming the deck never failed to make me smile. One day a chicken fell overboard. One of the crew, Glen, jumped in to save her but the rope tethering him (and the chook) to the boat broke and they both drifted away with the current. It was harrowing. We scoured the ocean for over half an hour and eventually, forty minutes into the search, we managed to find him, but he'd lost our meal. He said, "If that ever happens again I'm not going in after it. Fuck the chicken."

Stormy seas, drinking salt-contaminated water before Gan (AJT)

Politically speaking, a lot of people on board were anarchists or refugees from a system they rejected. One was an anti-European Union activist who later tried to blow up the European Union Parliament building in Brussels and served time in jail for it. There was also a film crew from French TV 4, doctors, lawyers, and various other professionals running away from mainstream society.

There were many personality clashes. Even though everyone was essentially on holiday, it wasn't always relaxing. One whom I shall call Camille saw herself as the boss, mostly because she organised fund-raising to keep the boat going. She thought very highly of herself, even putting down other original crew-members (and Niels) during meetings.

Our first stop in Sri Lanka was incredible. Intricately carved white stone temples, sandy white beaches teaming with wildlife, brightly-coloured Hindu mandirs (temples), lush tropical forests, deep green tea plantations hugging the soft hills and shops bursting with jewel-toned sari shops everywhere: it's a vibrant paradise. We hired a motorbike and spent a few days exploring the west coast of the country, zooming up to the highest point, Pidurutalagala Mountain, around five hours from the capital city, Colombo.

Maree left the boat in Sri Lanka and, as much as I wanted to stay longer, we were off again, to the Maldives. What should have been an easy journey of around a thousand kilometres was extremely hazardous.

Despite the problems on (and with) the boat, I felt safe with Niels as the captain. He was not only a very capable sailor with excellent navigational skills; he was able to easily smooth over any conflicts between the crew. He was the boat's peacemaker.

Crew-member Vincent Clouzeau, who was one of the two original champions of the construction of *La Dame de Canton* along with Niels back in the late 1970s, helped promote the boat's adventures by inviting

*Jean-Louis, Niels, Cala Vicuña, a noted Chilean surfer, and
Claude raising the mainmast sails (AJT)*

*From left, Niels, Vincent, Marie-Noëlle-Lebouis, Eric Ollivier
(holding ship's cat) and Mary (AJT)*

advertising and film crews on board, and we were constantly bumping into cameras. I don't recall anyone ever writing a chapter in a book about our adventures on the junk. I believe this is the first time a chapter has been published. I believe that a video was made for a French Television documentary, and that a book or manuscript was rejected for publication in France.

One of my strongest memories from this time is that we were always naked. It took me a while to get used to being unclothed around strangers, and I can't remember why we were always nude, but that's just the way it was. No-one ever questioned it!

Our meals on board were at times amazing. Mary was an excellent cook: she was the type of person who could turn three old tins of beans and a can of soup into a gourmet meal. When we were running low on provisions we never had to worry about eating bland, crappy meals, and with all the fresh fish we caught along the way we ate well.

Our next destination was the tropical paradise of the Maldives. The Maldives were just like you'd expect them to be: stunning. Crystal clear waters teeming with colourful fish, empty glittering beaches littered with palm trees, and smooth soft grey boulders. I'd never seen such delicately-coloured rocks before: they looked like they were hand-painted. The Maldivian people were adorable. They're a predominantly Islamic nation that thrives on tourism, in a way that was genuine, friendly and beyond helpful. The locals helped us fix our boat and would do anything for cans of Coca-Cola. Coke was currency here: we could trade cola for chickens. Fortunately we had cases of the stuff on board so instead of using money, we bought supplies with soda.

Again, we weren't there long. What should have been a short trip to one of the Maldivian islands, Gan, was vile. Our freshwater somehow got mixed up with the saltwater and we all got sick. Then we ran out of food.

Even though Mary could cook up anything she needed to start with basic ingredients, and all we had was rice and salty water. We all got sick and the seas were rough. Expending a lot of energy without boosting our bodies' reserves made for a very difficult time. Plus, we got lost in cloudy weather. Navigation in those days was by sextant, compass and chronometer. The only way to know where you were at sea was to make regular, timed observations of the angles of the sun and the stars, in ways that would have been completely familiar to Captain Cook. It was still few years before the coming of 'modern times' in the form of satellite navigation!

And so till the skies cleared we literally just floated around, hoping not to be driven onto rocks or a rough coast by the winds and waves and shipwrecked. Being lost on land is scary — being lost at sea is terrifying.

The deck leaked so all our bedding got wet, and of course when you're in a storm there's no sunlight to dry everything out, either. We were not only scared but also hungry, cold, sick, wet, and tired as well.

We eventually found our way to Gan, a desert island with an abandoned RAF airstrip. Even though no-one lived there — which is the meaning of the phrase 'desert island', short for deserted — it was a meeting place for other voyagers. We met people from all over the world on Gan, all of whom were either anarchists or socialists. While we were there, Mary Budgen, the youthful mother and cook of the boat, and Jean-Louis Couderc, the ship's mechanic and electrician and supervisor of its construction got married. Niels was their celebrant.

In spite of all the other visitors, Niels and I tried to go ashore to spend a few days alone on Gan. Without a tent or anything to sleep under we had to make do. We found a piece of corrugated iron, which served as a roof, and we slept on the ground in a sleeping bag. Our romantic scheme was to catch fish and cook it over a fire. But every time Niels hooked one, a shark appeared out of nowhere and grabbed it before he could get it out of the water!

Sharks love to devour hooked fish, an easy if unsporting meal. The struggles of the doomed creature somehow telegraph to any patrolling shark that it cannot get away: and there was obviously no shortage of sharks near Gan. Even climbing coconut trees for fresh fruit was a disaster as we couldn't get up the trees! Climbing a coconut tree is one of those things more easily seen, than done.

So, on an exotic desert island, we survived on canned fish that we could have bought at the supermarket at home. Despite the challenges, we were the happiest we'd ever been together, even when we realised that our sleeping bag was on a nest of scorpions.

Elf-Chine was pretty smashed up by this stage, already, so the crew decided to try and get it fixed at Diego Garcia, the largest of a group of islands south of the Maldives known as the Chagos Archipelago. Diego Garcia was a top-secret American military base (it still is). Though the Chagos Archipelago is part of the British Indian Ocean Territory, its heavy American presence suggests that both the USA and Britain have an interest in maintaining a presence there.

Diego Garcia was home to the Chagossians, native people of the Chagos Archipelago who were forcibly removed when the base was constructed in the late 1960s. They've been trying to get their land back ever since and Vincent Clouzeau started representing them after we left in 1982. Amal Clooney, actor George Clooney's wife, is currently suing the America Government to return the land to the Chagossians.

Certain members of the crew declared an emergency over the radio so that we would be welcomed into the port. Our problems were somewhat over-dramatised in order to make sure that the Americans would let us in. To be honest I wondered, even then, whether some people on the junk secretly wanted to film the military base as well.

These days, there's not much that's hidden from Google Earth / Satellite. But back then, Diego Garcia might as well have been on the moon. Its secret-squirrel status undoubtedly piqued people's curiosity.

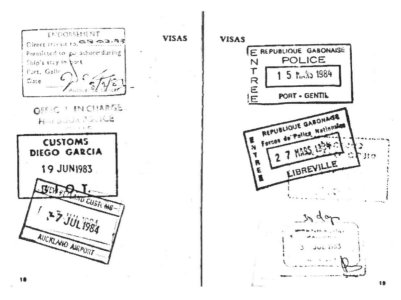

Diego Garcia stamp in my passport—not many people have that

The Americans were fantastic — they helicoptered food to us. Seeing hamburgers and other food lowered from a navy chopper was one of the craziest things I'd experienced up till then. Actually the Americans had done the same thing when the *Elf-Chine* was in the South China Sea early in 1982 before I joined the crew, so they were probably keeping track of us too.

I was very upset with the crew members who I felt had lied to the Americans, and to me. I didn't like being part of what felt like a conspiracy

Above: Maree, on the junk

Top left: Neils and I cross-dressing on the junk, probably for a crossing-the-line party

Left: me looking sultry on the island of Gan

The Canton Lady leaves Hong Kong under full bamboo sail. At sea (left), her crew work hard to stay shipshape. But they get time off, with clothes off, like Aussie Glenn Antruss (centre), a recent addition to the party.

What a high time on the high seas: from Canton to Paris in a Chinese junk built for adventure

THE GREAT JUNK

People *magazine (Australia), courtesy* Bauer Media Group

JAUNT

WHEN 10 people decide to sail halfway around the world they're looking for adventure all right. And when they go by Chinese junk, adventure finds them.

More than two years ago the Canton Lady, a graceful old junk fitted with special bamboo sails for extra seaworthiness, began a voyage across the South China Sea and the Indian Ocean with a crew of 10 Europeans.

No sooner had they left behind the Chinese port of Canton, bound for Paris, than they sailed into nearby Hong Kong and a boat shelter preparing for a typhoon. They left the colony before it hit, but three days out, en route to the Philippines, it caught them.

Rain and winds of 60 knots buffeted the junk, visibility was reduced to nil, and the crew feared they wouldn't survive their first experience of an awesome typhoon.

But they did — and so did their boat. Yet when the storm cleared, danger of another sort awaited on an overnight stop off the Philippines coast. The crew awoke to find themselves bailed up by an ominous band of Filipinos brandishing firearms. Pirates, they shuddered, murderers who profit by looting and sinking Vietnamese boats and selling women into prostitution and slavery.

Luckily they were wrong. The leader of the band stepped forward and identified himself and his men as police. It was a case of double mistaken identity: they thought the junk was carrying boat people.

This happened again going to Singapore via Malaysia. Until the authorities knew there were no Vietnamese refugees on board, they kept the crew at gunpoint.

In Singapore, the crew grew with Australian Glenn Anfruss and New Zealander Jenny Walker, who at 21 was the youngest. Also on board was a lovely 25-year-old British-Chinese girl who had fallen in love with the boat — and its Basque mechanic.

The Canton Lady sailed across the Indian Ocean via Sri Lanka and the Maldives. The next destination was Mauritius, but 200 kilometres from the islands in the Chagos archipelago, they encountered such bad weather that the crew had to turn back. This time they pulled in to the island of Diego-Garcia, which houses a British-US military base and therefore discourages distressed vessels.

However the crew were allowed four days to complete repairs, working in round-the-clock shifts.

The next attempt at reaching Mauritius was more successful although the weather was no better on the way. On arrival they hit the first open bar — and started plotting their next bound-for-Paris leg.

and there were tensions on board. Four crew members left, and one of the people who'd reported the 'emergency' was the one who ended up being arrested years later for trying to blow up the European Parliament.

Our next brief stop was Mauritius, a small though extraordinarily heavily populated island nation east of Madagascar. Independent from Britain since 1968, Mauritius has one and a quarter million inhabitants on a total land area of about two thousand square kilometres. Thus if you imagine Auckland, plus a bit of the surrounding countryside and the smaller Hauraki Gulf Islands, all cut out with a cookie cutter and relocated hundreds of kilometres out in the ocean, that is roughly what Mauritius is like.

In Mauritius, we got raided. Our boat was searched for drugs and guns and, even though someone had a half-marijuana, half-tobacco cigarette on the table under a stack of paper, they still didn't find anything. We were lucky. Some of the crew went and tried African marijuana which was super strong. I watched them smoke a tiny flake and they were high. The fear of being busted overseas was enough to make me stay away from smoking pot. Even if it was decriminalised in New Zealand, I wouldn't smoke it.

We headed to South Africa to get the boat repaired. I got off the boat for three weeks to meet up with my father whom I hadn't seen for almost two years. After spending a few days catching up, we headed to the Kruger National Park. Standing in an open-roofed vehicle overlooking the African savannah teeming with giant creatures was surreal, like being in a movie. Giraffes and elephants seem to be twice the size you expect. Even zebras are monstrous. It was survival of the fittest I guess.

Being in South Africa at the height of its oppression, when I'd been such a fierce anti-apartheid campaigner, was sickening. Seeing "whites only" signs was incredibly distressing. One of our French crew members, a black man, was kicked out of the local swimming pool because he was swimming in

Playing Music and Dancing from La Réunion to Mauritius *(AJT)*

the white-only part. They told him that he was only allowed to swim at the other end of the pool in a tiny sectioned off part with a sign saying "non-whites only." As upsetting as that was, it was nothing compared to the disgusting racist conversations I overheard every day. Afrikaner racism made New Zealand racism pale in comparison (it was the law after all).

It made my skin crawl, especially in Johannesburg. Even going to the movie theatre was revolting, Afrikaners almost having sex on the seats and shouting abuse at anyone on screen that was non-white. Cape Town wasn't as bad. If I'd had to choose one place to live in South Africa it would be Cape Town: at least it's a pretty city.

Some of our crew started filming a documentary and invited anti-apartheid activist Allan Boesak on board. Years later, Boesak would be appointed by Nelson Mandela to represent South Africa at the United Nations in Geneva. Listening to Allan's stories was fascinating and utterly heart-breaking. That was still seven years before Mandela was released and eleven before he became President.

Worried about the perils I was getting into, my father begged me to return to New Zealand. I decided to think about it, while still travelling of course.

We left South Africa and began the long journey up the coast to Gabon, a small but lush French-speaking country on the west coast of central Africa. Before we arrived, it was foggy and we had to use lights and our horn. After months of punishment at sea the mainmast broke: but luckily it did so only thirty nautical miles out of Libreville, the capital city and main port of Gabon. I had to jump overboard with other crew members to cut the cable holding the mast to the junk and secure it to the side. Luckily the water was calm.

S. N. Elf-Aquitaine, the French petroleum company that sponsored the journey, paid us some more money to film commercials off the oil rigs. They filmed the junk sailing past the oil rigs: they liked the contrast of old and new technology I guess. They also invited us to a remote island off the coast for dinner. It was a bizarre evening, travelling to an abandoned house on an island in the middle of nowhere. I didn't feel comfortable going, but because there were around thirty of us I figured there was safety in numbers.

We arrived at the derelict farmhouse to find the patio filled with tables set for a silver service dinner: crisp white linen tablecloths, elegantly-dressed waiters and tantalising gourmet smells coming from the kitchen. The meal was exquisite; duck drowning in rich velvety sauces, enough seafood to feed an army and beautiful wines from all over France. But the petroleum executives were rude, obnoxious and full of their own self-importance, ordering the waiters around, clicking and snapping their fingers for attention and constantly yelling, "Garçon, garçon!"

* * *

I started to get homesick; I'd been on the junk for two years. I was craving land and needed to get away from the friction on board following the Diego Garcia incident. The other crew were also beginning to miss their homes and families. Mary was pregnant so wanted to head back to Paris to have her baby.

My mind was made up for me when Niels became very sick. He urgently needed an operation for a collapsed lung. We departed as soon as we could, saying goodbye to everyone and getting on the next plane bound for Paris.

We landed in Paris and I met my Niels' family including his mother Ariane and his grandmother Lilette, a colourful character. Ariane was a petite, classy, romantic woman. She'd had five husbands and had written a book about why women should have toy-boys. Niels' paternal grandfather Charles was an arty gentleman, raised in a manor with servants. Charles Lutyens joined a motorcycle club in New York in the 1950s, became a radical artist in the 60s and was now a charismatic patron of the arts. He occasionally still dabbled in art, but suffered from paralysis by over-analysis, so he never actually finished anything. He'd been working on a sculpture of Jesus' face for three years!

We stayed with Niels' brother Paul and got fat on brie, wine and the deep sounds of underground jazz. The music scene in Paris in the 1980s was out of this world: the musicians, the decor, the trumpeters, the singing, it was a decadent period and I loved it. It made me realise how much I missed home and I decided it was time to go.

After I left, the junk had a change of crew and journeyed to the United States and other destinations around the Caribbean, and was sold to its current owner in 1995, with the original association that built it still having a minority small interest. Since then, as I mentioned earlier, the boat has been tied up on the River Seine, serving as a restaurant and entertainment venue.

Sadly, my departure from Paris meant my relationship with Niels ended as well. To this day I still think that jumping on a Chinese junk and travelling the world would be something I'd love to do again, although maybe with clothes this time.

CHAPTER TWO

Maverick Beginnings

I have always been a maverick. A renegade. A free spirit. I have been travelling since the age of four.

Back then, it was usually to the local park thirty minutes away. Sometimes, I'd be accompanied by my younger brother and sister whom I'd squash into a pram and drag along with me. My mother always knew where to find me. She'd just follow the footsteps in the frost. No-one ever knew how I managed to navigate my way there: clearly I had a penchant for travel.

At ten I joined the Labour Party. I'd been raised with a sense of social justice. My father was an anti-war activist and successful campaign manager for the Local Labour Party in Hastings, and my uncle John once carried a pig's head on stick at a protest, to demonstrate his annoyance with the then New Zealand Prime Minister Robert 'Piggy' Muldoon's policies.

At the age of eleven I travelled by myself to Wellington with Halt All Racist Tours (HART), a protest group that picketed visiting South African sports teams. I clearly remember being incensed by apartheid and racism as a pre-teen. So, I joined a local HART group and marched alongside adults protesting a visit by the South African softball team. It wasn't long before police started tapping the family phone. It was pretty common to have undercover listeners in those days.

As a twelve-year-old I started dressing creatively. I showcased my efforts every Sunday at church. I wore string around my feet instead of shoes, which I paired with a floor-length hippy dress and a crocheted headband tied around my forehead.

In my fourteenth year I was determined to see Labour Prime Minister Norman Kirk's funeral procession. Kirk had died suddenly in office at the age of only fifty-one. I just had to see him, I'd always admired him.

I was in Christchurch at the time of the funeral and the only member

My grandparents from Dundee: Mary Edwards Greig and Johnny Walker

My parents' engagement: Brian Walker and Judy Anne Kessell

of my Hastings Hockey Team to brave the bad weather; even though it was pouring with rain. I was the only kid amongst a sea of adults paying their respects.

When I was fourteen I was expelled from my first of two schools. School One: for getting involved in the abortion controversy. School Two: for delivering a speech on how Communism and Catholicism are interrelated. Other children's speeches were of a lighter nature, like the differences between marmite and vegemite.

On my fifteenth birthday I started work at the local freezing works. The day after my fifteenth birthday I stopped working at the local freezing works and became a vegetarian. The smell of bovine fear mixed with blood and urine was something that traumatised me for years. It was nearly a decade before I ate meat again.

Fifteen was a big year for me clothing-wise; I discovered punk. My hippy dressing years were over. I had seven studs in my ears, one in my nose and wore a bright yellow jumpsuit, riddled with safety pins.

At sixteen I told my parents I supported the decriminalisation of marijuana, and lit up a joint in front of them. They said nothing. I guess they thought it was one of the least damaging things I'd done at this stage.

When I turned seventeen I decided I'd never wear a bra, after reading Germaine Greer's comments on how tight underwear symbolised male oppression.

At eighteen I became obsessed with Bob Marley — the music, his activism and his love of the bud. My friend Robin and I hitchhiked to Auckland to see him in concert. I wore my hair in bright green dreadlocks, decorated with silver milk bottle tops. Our experimentation with pot became common knowledge; we were busted smoking dope by my friend's parents in news coverage of the concert.

To top off my last year as a child, I kicked a nuclear-powered submarine. I was with an anti-nuke organisation protesting American nuclear-powered ships in our ports when I jumped on a protest boat, driven by none other than soon-to-be mayor, Tim Shadbolt. We headed out into the ocean to vocalise our displeasure at the United States nuclear ship Truxtun and I got close enough to kick it!

So, where did I get my moxie from?

Hastings felt like a small town in the sixties. With a population of twenty-three thousand there were really only two career options available: working with cows or working with fruit.

Not the most exciting choices for a maverick-in-the-making (it's no surprise I left Hastings as soon as I could).

Growing up we spoke in a Scottish dialect — Dundonian. I just assumed that every other family spoke it too. I didn't realise that we were any different,

Myself with siblings Lawrie and Maree Walker

but we were.

My mother was a Roman Catholic-cum-hippy who later became a Jehovah's Witness. A stylish, softly-spoken teetotaller who loved animals and the outdoors, mum was the kind of woman birds would flock to when she strolled through the woods, just like St Francis (a little bit, at any rate). She loved birds so much: she'd breed them and change their colour by introducing natural dyes into their food. She was a speaker of Māori and rode a horse bareback. She was quietly adventurous. I definitely inherited the adventurous part.

* * *

Incidentally, you might ask why I put a line above the letter 'a' in Māori. This is a new spelling innovation which came in about a generation ago to render the spelling of Māori words more phonetic, and as far as possible I stick to it. The line on top, the 'macron', means that a vowel is stressed and lengthened — as if saying *Maaori* — and to double the vowel is another way of indicating the same change in pronunciation, though less common these days now that the macron has come in.

Some Māori words can have several meanings depending on whether a vowel is stressed in this way or not, as with tones in languages like Chinese or Vietnamese. Thus the word 'ata' can have three completely different and unrelated meanings depending on whether the first 'a' is stressed, the second, or neither. But that is an extreme case and in general the issue is less critical in Māori than in languages that have a fully developed tone system. This also makes Māori less complicated to write in a Romanised system than, say, Vietnamese, since there is only one change to mark on the top of a vowel letter and not several.

It was not until quite recently that Māori spelling reflected the issue at all. The spelling of Māori words on road signs, in official place names and most publications still does not include the macron. If I am quoting from a source that does not use the macron, including place names in current and common use without macrons, or people's names from the past, I will not bother to officiously correct such words (and risk getting them wrong) but just use them as I have seen them.

* * *

All of my friends were welcome at our house because my mother always made everybody feel welcome. There was never anybody excluded: my mother was a very warm person indeed. Our house was always open to our friends.

My Scottish father was a welder, democratic socialist, trade unionist and an avid Association Football (soccer) fan. He was somewhat swarthy in appearance in his younger days and figured that he had Spanish ancestry to account for it. Everybody in the wilder parts of Britain and Ireland can trace their ancestry to a shipwrecked sailor of the Spanish Armada, or so it seems: and Dad was no exception.

He answered to the nickname of 'Arab' or 'the Aberdeen Arab'. Small-town New Zealand wasn't particularly accepting of people with a non-definable look in the 1970s. Dad's appearance confused the locals, not to mention the distinction between Dundee and Aberdeen. His staunch anti-war views and political activism rubbed off on me from a young age.

One of my earliest political memories was listening to Education Minister Phil Amos—we actually became besties later on in life when we were both on the Auckland City Council—and Māori Affairs Minister Matiu Rata, who years later gave me two hours of his time to discuss socialism. I was shocked by media perceptions of him: even as a fifteen- year-old I'd begun to see through the veneer of mainstream media. Matiu was an inspiring and intelligent leader, yet he was portrayed as a simpleton who couldn't read. I found it infuriating.

My Uncle John was in the Boilermakers Union and knocked a guy out when he called him a Pom. That was yet another ethnic slur in circulation at the time, for recent arrivals from Britain in this case, which some said was short for Prisoners of Mother England. He was Scottish.

Clearly, activism and adventure were in my blood. So, after finishing school or rather school finishing with me, I moved to New Zealand's biggest city, Auckland.

CHAPTER THREE

Rest Homes aren't Restful Places

MY first job was my worst job: cleaning toilets at a rest home. Sometimes I got to make the beds, a step up from being a bog-botherer. I realised pretty quickly that I was not a nurse-aid.

Auckland gave me a crash course in a side of life I'd never have known in Hastings. I was staying with a friend from school whose parents ran a rather notorious pub at the end of Hobson Street.

At that time, inner-city Auckland wasn't the cosmopolitan hub of café culture that it was later to become. It was run-down and seedy and had a huge hard-drug problem. The ambience of the area was reflected in the songs of gritty urban bands like Dragon (a reference to heroin) and Hello Sailor (a reference to something else), not to mention their names.

The hotel I was living at — and I use the term 'hotel' loosely — was where all the junkies, sailors drinking vodka with milk and pill-popping transvestites lived. It wasn't the fact that they were transvestites that bothered me; it was the pill-popping.

(My mum used to grade apples in the orchards and would sometimes bring glamorous transvestites over for dinner: she loved the long painted nails and fashionable denim skirts. I think she just liked being around beautiful-looking people. So, that wasn't the problem...)

Every night I'd get home from work and literally run through the pub, down the long hallway and up three flights of stairs, sometimes in the dark because the lights didn't always work, and into my room where I'd lock the door. Instantly. Even when I was safely in my room I still felt unsettled: for the place seemed to be haunted as well. I felt that there were other people living there. You could hear and sense them walking around at night. I've always wondered whether the fact that it was reclaimed land made it spookier.

My job at the rest home didn't work out. I was made redundant. I didn't see myself staying in the 'industry'. I headed back to Hastings to finish my high school education and sit my University Entrance exam, a year later than most. I sat it and passed it, and immediately hitchhiked back to Auckland to start my tertiary education.

CHAPTER FOUR

Phone Taps and Lots of Scraps

THE 1970s was a frightening time in New Zealand. Under the authoritarian rule of Prime Minister Robert 'Piggy' Muldoon, everyone in the Labour Party, HART or nuclear disarmament movements in New Zealand was seen as a virus. In later years friends of mine had their police files released and were shocked to see the level of surveillance on all of us — photos at various protest marches over the years and complete transcripts of conversations. Disagreeing with the paranoid government meant in-depth interference; they weren't used to being confronted.

Every time we protested, the Security Intelligence Service (SIS) would show up, always wearing yellow tee-shirts and short blue shorts: the security service in stubbies.

The house I flatted in kept getting busted by the police: our house was searched every day for a month. Our household of student flatmates was known to the cops as being protest headquarters for anti-apartheid, anti-nuclear power and pro-abortion rallies; if there was a civil rights or social issue to protest, we were front and centre. The SIS never found anything. I'm not sure what they were really expecting to find at a broke students' flat.

We knew when our phones were being tapped because they'd ring randomly without anyone on the other end, and there was a clicking sound during phone calls. During a call we would sometimes hear random breaths and noises that interrupted our conversations.

The protests over the 1981 tour by the South African rugby team, the Springboks, the largest and most disruptive of the time, served as a particular reminder that not all was well in Aotearoa, the Māori name for New Zealand, which is often used as an alternative, especially by those sympathetic to indigenous peoples.

Members of other families were fighting each other over their viewpoints at the time of the 1981 Springbok Tour — but not mine. My family were united in their opposition to the tour, and growing up as lovers of Association Football (soccer), not rugby fanatics, meant that we were one step removed from the sport altogether.

The day of the tour my brother and I joined the Biko Squad section of the anti-Springbok protest movement. During the protests each squad was named after a prisoner or famous anti-apartheid activist. The Biko Squad was named after Steve Biko, an activist who had been beaten up by police while being detained in the South African city of Port Elizabeth in 1977.

After Steve Biko started to get worse from his injuries, the police made the strangely ill-advised decision to drive him overnight to a prison hospital in the city of Pretoria, roughly a thousand kilometres away by road. And so Biko spent vital hours bumping around on the floor of a police Land Rover as it trundled all night through the rural back-blocks of South Africa. Soon after arriving, he died.

Tragic, callous, and at the same time memorably bizarre, the incident made world headlines at the time. A song about Steve Biko was included on Peter Gabriel's third album in 1980: it's still well worth a listen.

We'd trained with wooden armour and helmets, ready for real confrontation. On the day, the police used their batons against people dressed as bumblebees, breaking collarbones and arms. My brother retrieved a baton — I wonder if he's still got it?

In these protests things really did get quite disruptive and out of hand in ways that seem incredible now. I threw lit firecrackers at the Police. Ironically the fact that the New Zealand Police don't carry sidearms, that those were somewhat more innocent times and that we don't really have much a gun culture in New Zealand — we are like Britain in that respect — meant that that wasn't alarming as it sounds, since everyone knew it was just firecrackers. Still, it shows that there is a pretty thin veneer of civilisation at times, and that it is best not to put it under too much strain.

* * *

If I might digress once more for a moment, this is a good opportunity to talk about what the lovely name Aotearoa means. The exact meaning of Māori place-names is often mysterious, much as the origins of the name of an English village might not be clear either. In modern Māori 'Ao' means cloud, daytime or world; '-tea-' in the middle of a word means bright; and 'roa' means long. But also, 'aotea' is plausibly a contraction of 'awatea', meaning dawn.

In some tales, the name comes from the first sighting of the looming landmass of New Zealand by the wife or daughter of the legendary explorer Kupe. This woman or girl is supposed to have called out "He ao! He ao!", "A cloud! A cloud!", from which comes the common (and very free) translation 'land of the long white cloud'.

The lexicographer Harry Orsman, among others, took the view that what Aotearoa really refers to is a quality of long dawns and long twilights in New Zealand's latitudes, compared to the tropics where the sun rises and sets suddenly.

Firm proof that the name Aotearoa existed prior to the colonial period remains elusive. Captain Cook describes the North and South Islands as Eaheinomauwe and Toai Poonamoo, or in more modern spelling Te-Ika-a-Māui, the fish of Māui (the same Maui as in Hawai'i), and Te Waipounamu, the waters or place of greenstone (jadeite), respectively. The 1835 Declaration of Independence of the United Tribes of New Zealand and the 1840 Treaty of Waitangi made use of Māori transliterations of the English words New Zealand in their Māori-language texts and don't mention Aotearoa either.

It seems likely that, as a name for all of New Zealand, Aotearoa arose in the nineteenth century as a sort of 'invented tradition' of the sort that are often associated with the emergence of new nations and the formalisation, codification and writing-down of their culture. The classic case of the invented tradition is the close and pedantic identification of specific Scottish tartans with specific clans. The tartan system only became completely cut-and-dried once popular encyclopaedias and guides began to be written about clans and tartans in the nineteenth century.

As a new name for the land of the Māori to compete with the name bestowed upon it by its European colonisers, Aotearoa certainly sounds better than the transliterations of New Zealand that were used in Māori to begin with, such as Nu Tirani. But even in the later part of the nineteenth century Aotearoa was often still only being used as an alternative name for the North Island, specifically. It took time to be generally accepted as applying to the whole country, and ironically enough it might be said that the final push came with the 1898 publication of *The Long White Cloud / Ao-Tea-Roa* by the Christchurch-born social reformer and politician William Pember Reeves, a Pākehā or European New Zealander.

The likely meaning of Aotearoa reminds me of a remark by J. R. R. Tolkien's friend and fellow author C. S. Lewis, who wrote in his autobiography *Surprised by Joy* of an imagined sub-Arctic realm free of industrial pollution, of "pure 'northernness'. . . a vision of huge, clear spaces hanging above the Atlantic in the endless twilight." Though it is much closer to the equator New Zealand still doubles for such a landscape today, whence the fact that this country served as a backdrop to movies made from Tolkien's fantasy-books.

And so I like to think that the word Aotearoa, even or perhaps especially if invented sometime in the nineteenth century by Māori nationalists now unknown along with its subsequent appropriation by Pākehā like Reeves, *does* refer to a sort of southerly analogue of Lewis's 'northernness', a forerunner of today's notions of 'clean green' or '100% Pure' New Zealand.

* * *

Getting back to my own story, I enrolled in Auckland University with the aim of doing law, but quickly changed my subject when a professor said that "By the time you've finished at Law School you'll be able to fill these forms in without any help." I didn't want to study just so I could learn to fill out forms!

The only good thing about University was meeting a man called Wu Zhao Yi, the first Chinese Communist to be allowed to study in New Zealand. I met him quite randomly on campus one day and we developed a friendship. Everywhere we went, we got free meals. He'd introduce himself to the Chinese owners and there would never be any bill at the end of our meals; so I ate free for about six months.

Wu and I went to see the Chinese football team play the All Whites in 1982. Even though New Zealand won the game and advanced to the 1982 World Cup, there was almost a riot when we left the grounds. All Whites fans were running around making slit-eye signs and shouting horrible racial slurs. I was disgusted and disheartened by the blatant racism.

I didn't last long at University. Two months of it and I was bored. Bored of everyone protesting, ironically enough — I'd been doing it since I was ten years old and I needed a break!

I dropped out of University, got a job and moved back into my friend's parents' place, the dodgy haunted hotel. I worked in the local and international exchange connecting calls and I loved it. The hours were long but I loved the people I worked with and the money of course. I remember saving NZ$9,200 in eighteen months, in the currency of the time. That was amazing money to make for a twenty-year-old without a degree back then.

I could not wait to leave New Zealand. Like many New Zealanders, including many among the million or so New Zealanders who live overseas, I felt absolutely alienated and that I could not breathe free unless I was somewhere else. Looking back, this was surely another source for my wanderlust.

I decided I did not enjoy the education system. I felt that my individuality was suppressed. I couldn't politically express myself either at school or through clothing without being ostracised. I was becoming an angry person and just frustrated with it all.

I was sick of constantly watching rugby and seeing the national rugby team, the All Blacks treated like heroes when there were real heroes we should have been celebrating instead. I was tired of being followed around by the police and the Security Intelligence Service.

I was tired of everything. I'd had enough. I felt that New Zealand was a divided society to live in. I couldn't wait to go.

So, I left New Zealand with my sister Maree.

CHAPTER FIVE

Ciao New Zealand

MAREE and I moved to Sydney, my first time overseas. I was desperate to have a break from New Zealanders.

We settled in Bondi, not realising that's where all the New Zealanders lived! It was just like being at home. On my twenty-first birthday I had a car accident on the Sydney Harbour Bridge and had to pay hundreds of dollars to fix both cars. Happy birthday to me!

Maree and I decided to head to Darwin, the most northern city in Australia and one of the hottest.

I got a job in the local casino. I had never done bar work before and I had to learn how, quick smart. I managed to get myself sorted within the first week and got paid very good money, but I hated it. The men would sometimes drink four dozen bottles of beer over weekend and even keep it up for longer. This was called 'going troppo', meaning they were affected by the tropical heat. They would say openly racist things like "I'm going to run over a boong on the way home". Boong was a derogatory term the white Australians would use for the Aboriginals, the native people of Australia.

Darwin was a sad place. Lots of white men would bring Aboriginal women to the Casino and try to get them drunk.

One time I got into trouble with my manager because I refused to give these girls alcohol because they didn't want it - they only wanted fizzy drinks. I remember the men were just trying to make them drunk so they would be less likely to refuse their sexual advances. It was revolting.

While we were in Darwin I made friends with some local Aboriginal girls, they were all about the same age as me.

We would talk a lot and they told me shocking stories of their childhoods. They'd been separated from their mothers when they were little because they were half white Australian and half Aboriginal. They were only allowed to see their mums and families through wire fences, no physical contact was allowed. It was truly heart-breaking stuff. Most of them were put into welfare homes, or adopted to non-Aboriginal families. I remember thinking how absolutely awful that would have been for them. We got invited to watch them play the didgeridoo one night, a traditional Aboriginal musical instrument. That was great to watch and we stayed for three hours!

I became close friends with an Aboriginal guy named Allan and was hauled into the manager's office at the Casino. Apparently you weren't allowed to have Aboriginal friends AND work in the casino. I told the Casino that if they were going to dictate who my friends were they could get fucked. And I left.

My sister and I decided to get out of Darwin and go in to the outback. The outback of Australia is really remote, untainted by people and full of life. It was teeming with lizards, crocodiles, kangaroos and birds. And *bugs*. There were hundreds of them. The cockroaches were the size of small mice. I hated them with a passion — love the outback, hate the bugs.

We had met some other travellers from Greece and Italy, so they came with us out to Kakadu National Park. We were told we had to look out for crocodiles in the water. But of course we went and swam in swimming holes we shouldn't have. One day while we were mucking about on a small boat and toboggan we saw something lurking around in the water not that far away from us. The splashing and noise had sparked the interest of a three-metre long croc. I was scared, but luckily we were still far enough away to be able to make a quick exit.

My experiences in Darwin ruined my impression of Australia. The bugs were revolting. I don't want to live in a country where the cockroaches are as big as mice, even if the country does have incredible seafood.

We decided that a round-the-world trip was the best option, so off we went.

CHAPTER SIX
Magic Vegetables in Indonesia

BALINESE people are beautiful. Personality-wise, and looks-wise. But the country, in those days, was full of drugs.

On the trip with my sister we found that you could get magic mushrooms in omelettes, in soups, in salads, even in your vodka. Everyone was eating (or drinking) something hallucinogenic in Bali.

Being young and adventurous, Maree and I tried some of these mushrooms, and we hallucinated so badly that she wanted to become a nun. I had to spend about six or seven hours calming her down. She spoke in tongues and was speaking in a weird language, it sounded like Thai to me. My mother and grandmother could speak in tongues, but I always thought they just sounded drunk. So I've seen first-hand people speaking in tongues in a religious and hallucinogenic setting.

I was amazed at the Hindu culture there. As we walked around the streets we had to be watching our step. The Balinese would place all these little offerings on the footpaths, flowers, crackers and even cigarettes. I didn't want to offend anyone by stepping on one.

Mosquitoes were a big problem in Bali. The Balinese people told us that if you drink black tea it would keep them away — apparently it's a natural repellent.

After that, my sister and I met a group of men from Jakarta who were students. They loved Phil Collins and they were playing songs from his

album, *Yes*. We had a great time with them and singing along to Mr Collins.

Maree and I left Bali and flew to Medan in the north of Indonesia. Tourists were a rarity here. Medan was under-developed and unable to accommodate visitors. As we didn't speak the language, we were playing hit and miss with ordering food.

That ended badly, I remember thinking that the beef I'd ordered tasted old and tough. What I didn't realise is that we were eating an animal that was a pet in a lot of New Zealand homes. It was only afterwards that I double-checked what we'd ordered from the butcher's window. Sure enough, it was a dog jaw.

It made me feel sick. And then it made me actually sick with dysentery. If you've never had it, be very thankful. I lost 9 kilos in weight in under a fortnight. It was a seriously shit time.

The men here thought that rubbing strangers' breasts was okay, so I felt very unsafe! I'd never been groped so much before.

Our accommodation in Medan was hideous: dirty, dark, dingy hallways and prison cell-sized dorm rooms filled with cockroaches. No wonder it only cost one dollar a night. It wasn't a really safe place to travel in. Medan was memorable, but not for good reasons: leaving was the only option. It might be quite different now, of course!

Central Java had a completely different vibe. The stunning ornate stone temple at Borobudur, from the ninth century, took me instantly to a bygone era. Having grown up in the Catholic Church this was a very different form of worship for me. Especially as there were thousands of bats hiding amongst the ruins, fruit for the gods at every corner, incense sticks burning and the remnants of recent chicken sacrifices.

I loved this area so much I stayed for three months. I moved into a flat with a friend of a friend who was in a rock band, and was chauffeured around by a driver that my friend shared with the Japanese ambassador. They were fun times. Except for being mistaken as a prostitute everywhere I went.

In those days, white women were seen and treated like they were hookers. Whenever I went out with my friend Tony, men used to approach him asking if they could have a "turn" with me. And because we were driving around with a chauffeur they thought I could just service them in the car.

But it wasn't just my skin colour that drew stares and comments. Maree used to attract crowds because she had lots of joined-together freckles on her face. Children used to try and swipe them. Even if we were zooming past them on a moped!

I went back to Bali a few years later on my own, and it was then that I met my good friend Ina. It is quite a funny story actually. We met each other while out exploring one day, two young ladies out on an adventure: it was all a lot of fun. We stayed in this one hotel and the manager there thought he could try and hit on us. He harassed us to no end to get in to bed with him, to the point we weren't going to stay there anymore. We were so disgusted, so before we did leave we thought we'd play a little trick on him. We found a condom and filled it with shampoo and left it on the bed and then promptly left the hotel. Just to piss him off. We still laugh about it even to this day!

When I was in Medan with Maree, Tony asked me to marry him; but he was Islamic and I would have to convert to that religion. I wasn't sure that was my cup of tea. That was my cue to leave Indonesia to the next destination.

CHAPTER SEVEN

Mmm Malaysia

W E flew from Jakarta to Singapore. I loved how modern and clean Singapore was. A completely welcome experience considering the ones Maree and I had just had.

We only spent a couple of nights in Singapore. I had planned to do a tramp through a National Park in Malaysia. So we caught the next flight to Kuala Lumpur.

I grew up outdoors and I'd always loved tramping. My mother used to take me to all the National Parks when I was a kid. So, the prospect of tramping in the Malaysian jungle was beyond exciting.

I'd arranged to be part of a thirty-day excursion staying in small tramper-style huts. We had to carry our own food and backpacks, which for thirty days was quite a heavy task.

Tramping in the Malaysian National Park of Taman Negara is quite different to Hawkes Bay. For a start, I'd never had to contend with leeches, which I learnt to burn off with lit cigarettes. The indigenous people in this area, known as Orang Asli, taught us to cover our bodies with tobacco to prevent ticks and other bugs nestling in.

Most tourist trampers were day-walkers, so being the only New Zealander in the jungle was a novelty. But nothing compared to seeing tiger footprints in the jungle or learning Malay which is very similar to the New Zealand Māori language. We spent our nights under the tree canopy singing and dancing, learning the traditional Malay dances.

Penang was next on the list and after an eight-hour bus ride in humid conditions I couldn't wait to get there. But that anticipation was short-lived.

All the other guests retired to their hotel rooms in the evenings with lit candles. I couldn't work out why as the power seemed to be on. I asked the owner and, though he was reluctant to tell me, I badgered him. He opened up. I instantly wished that he hadn't!

"The other guests are heroin addicts and they use the candles to melt the heroin in spoons."

Excuse me?! I was above and beyond shocked.

I'd heard about the drug culture in Penang. A mother and son drug smuggler pair, Lorraine and Aaron Cohen, had recently been arrested and sentenced to life in prison in Penang. I could never have imagined that it would be so brazen and in my face. I saw a junkie inject heroin into his ankle, then his eye. He then asked if I wanted any but I said no and ran in the opposite direction.

To lighten the mood, I decided to play a prank on the guests. So, the next day, I bought some plastic poo in a shop and put them all over the chairs in the hotel. People would come in, sit down, see the poo, be disgusted and then move.

Maree and I were laughing about it, when I noticed a beautifully-dressed Frenchman walk into the room. He was the most stunning person I had ever seen in my life.

He looked at me and smiled. I could feel the redness of a blush all over my face. Here I was holding a plastic poo, not the sort of thing you want to be holding when you see the most attractive man you've ever seen, laughing hysterically and probably looking completely ridiculous.

It didn't deter him though: Niels Lutyens and I fell in love.

Almost instantly.

Niels invited Maree and myself to sail with him, and his sister, to Thailand. So of course we did.

CHAPTER EIGHT
Naked Body to Local Body

ARRIVING back was surreal. I had been away from home for three years and for most of it had been on a Chinese junk full of naked people.

At this stage of my life I had no career to speak of, so I decided to enrol in a journalism course. Soon after finishing my diploma, I did a placement at the *Whakatane Beacon*, a local newspaper based in the East Coast of the North Island. I did not realise that the former Manager of the New Zealand All Blacks rugby team was the owner. I didn't last there long. My first story was an anti-Springbok piece and my intellectual freedom was compromised. I moved to the *Thames Star*, where my first piece was about how disenfranchised Māori couldn't practice their culture. My "voice" wasn't appreciated there either and so after only three months, I left.

So, I headed to Auckland. I'd only been back in New Zealand for just a few months and I'd already moved twice. My second time at the University of Auckland was a welcoming experience, unlike my first time. I loved learning, and I loved studying New Zealand politics and the 1840 Treaty of Waitangi, by which New Zealand was first established as a British colony albeit with some restrictions on the right of the settlers to run roughshod over the Māori (restrictions that soon came to be ignored), for an eventual Bachelor of Arts with honours; after which, I would go on to do a Masters degree. Being familiar with Māori gave me an edge when it came to studying the Treaty.

I wasn't studying with a job in mind. I just wanted to learn about New Zealand and, as university was free back then, it didn't require a heavy financial outlay. It makes me sad that education costs so much nowadays, with students racking up tens of thousands of dollars for a tertiary education. Where's the incentive to study politics, or anything else that doesn't lead immediately to a meal ticket, if you have to pay for it?

I worked full time throughout my degree in order to make ends meet. I door-knocked for market research companies, cold-called for telemarketing firms, and had a summer job working in the University gardens. I met David and Hillary Shackleton, relatives of the famous Antarctic explorer Sir Ernest Shackleton. There's an old cliché that all New Zealanders are in some way or another descended from explorers, either from Captain Cook or from the legendary Māori navigator Kupe. In David's case it was almost literally true.

The Shackletons were stalwarts of the local Labour Party, high-minded Christians that tried to convert those around them. We were good friends but they were unsuccessful with my conversion.

While studying and working in odd jobs I lived in Western Springs, in a renovated garage near the Auckland Zoo. The neighbours would regularly bring over cooked meals — steak, potatoes, stews and lots of spinach. They took pity on me for being a broke student and, being a broke student, I was grateful for the free food!

My parents moved to Thames, a small coastal town in the Coromandel region of New Zealand. It was only about an hour and a half's drive from Auckland so I spent a lot of time with them: but things there had changed. Unemployment in the region was rife, especially amongst Māori.

It seemed that the David Lange-led Labour Government had a hidden agenda of privatising education, health and the railways and introduced user-pays in education, along with massive layoffs in a whole range of

My corporate billboard look

industries and public services. They sold the Bank of New Zealand (BNZ), which in my view was a major rip-off. It wasn't the New Zealand I knew, that's for sure.

Even so, I joined the Princes Street Branch of the Labour Party in 1988, where I met David Shackleton's son Brian. We ended up spending many years together in a relationship. Buying our first home together, which I eventually owned outright. Little did I know that buying a house would end up sending me down a different career path in later years. A seven-bedroom house in Kingsland soon ended up being worth a lot of money, and once I was on the investment property ladder I never really had to work again. For someone so steeped in social concerns this was an ironic turnout, but to be quite frank, this is the only kind of enterprise that New Zealand society rewards.

Being surrounded by Shackletons re-energised me into making a difference. So, I stood for the Auckland City Council in 1992, the same time I finished my Master's degree in Politics and History. By that stage the Labour Government had collapsed, the Labour Party itself splitting into three factions, one of them the left-wing New Labour Party.

My 1993 thesis on the formation of the New Labour Party was controversial due to its claims that *laissez-faire* ideologies had permeated the politics of the Labour Party, and that Helen Clark, who became Prime Minister under a later Labour-led coalition government and then went on to prominence at the United Nations, had been a fence-sitter for refusing to vote against the sale of the BNZ. I had hoped for it to be published as a book, but this never happened. Actually, it's hard to get anything published in New Zealand, where the market is small. The author of a classic history of New Zealand, Keith Sinclair, used to say that some of the best work on New Zealand history was to be found in unpublished theses, so maybe I am in good company.

The New Labour Party later joined forces with the Greens and some other parties to form the Alliance party, a real force in the 1990s, which almost overtook the old Labour Party. Four Alliance members were elected onto the Auckland City Council, one of them being myself.

I represented the Mount Albert Ward of the city along with Frank Ryan, a councillor from the more conservative Citizens & Ratepayers Association who had previously served as Mayor of Mount Albert City from 1968 until it became a ward of Auckland City in 1989. In addition to being a veteran of Auckland local body politics, Frank was the father of the actress Lucy Lawless, whom we were all shortly to hear about in the character of Xena the Warrior Princess.

In place of the Mount Albert City Council there was now the Mount Albert Community Board and between 1992 and 1995 the Board had a majority of Alliance members, though it didn't have much real power. Frank and I were on the Board as well as on the Council; the only other non-Alliance member of the Board was Ray Cody, a retired sports broadcaster and founder of Grey Power, a lobby group for pensioners.

Being on the Council was hard yakka. I fought to stop native trees from being cut down and saved many throughout Auckland. I helped get glyphosate weedkiller banned from residential streets; the Council used hot water thereafter, which is a much safer option. I was on the Arts Committee too. Working against, instead of alongside, conservative 'arts patrons' who treated me like a child was mentally draining.

The Hero Parade was a protest in support of the gay rights movement in New Zealand, a local version of the Sydney Mardi Gras. The Arts Committee vehemently opposed any festivals or parades promoting gay pride, so there were lots of arguments. Deputy Mayor David Hay was a born again Christian who led the resistance against the Hero Parade. I openly defied him by marching in the parade myself. I'm pretty sure I was the first councillor or politician to have done so.

I leaked confidential minutes to the media, because I believed the public had a right to know how their money was being spent, particularly on projects like the Aotea Centre. This was (and is) a dismal 1980s corporate convention centre not far from the aforementioned 1970s police station.

A similarly fortress-like façade and generally inward-focused nature helps to ensure that not much ever happens in the adjacent Aotea Square, a windswept parade-ground which could have been a much livelier sort of public space if the Council had ever had any sensitivity about such things.

In the Alliance we also stood against further motorway expansion, the sale of community housing, and the sale and expansion of the Auckland port. We wanted to make sure the Auckland waterfront was there for the people of the city to actually use. An expansion of dredging was never an option. It would kill our snapper and we wanted to preserve our harbour.

I was on the Council's Property Committee, advised by the very knowledgeable economist Gareth Morgan; he predicted the current housing crisis.

When I was on the council, I reacquainted myself with Chris Trotter, the Dunedin-based left-wing political commentator and editor of a magazine called *Political Review*. I loved his magazine; it provided a degree of analysis that I think is sadly missing in today's society. The contributors were fantastic — they were usually from the left of course, people like Keith Locke and the late Bruce Jesson, with whom I spent many afternoons speaking while I was at University. Chris moved up to Auckland in 1998 and I remember showing him around the underground music scene in Auckland. We spent hours on Karangahape Road listening to live music — anything from young rappers to female singer-songwriters.

The 1990s was an exciting time for music. We had access to sounds from every genre. I'd always been a fan of New Zealand music, from the intelligent mixture of punk and funk music of Split Enz, to the soulful and folksy sounds of Tumanako 'Prince Tui' Teka and the Māori Volcanics show-band. Prince Tui Teka himself used to date my neighbour in Hawke's Bay. He would often show up with his white station wagon, embellished with carvings.

When I lost my re-election bid by about 20 votes in 1995, I was frankly relieved. I'd poured everything into that job and after a three-year stint I was burnt out.

People thought I would be interested in a Parliamentary career, but I wasn't prepared to make the sacrifice, and I didn't want to work in a job where you were damned if you do, damned if you don't. Parliamentarians aren't really given any respect and as long as politicians are despised, you'll find that many good people are discouraged from running for Parliament.

I did go to one bitter contest for selection; everyone was at each other's throats, arguing and behaving like apes. I'd had enough.

It's not surprising that the travel bug bit again and I took off overseas.

CHAPTER NINE

Ahhh-Merica

I was nervous about going to the United States. I had a skewed opinion about their politics after all the anti-nuclear protesting I'd done over the years. But I always like to challenge my own perceptions of things, so thought an extended trip to America was needed to really learn about the country and its people.

Venice Beach in California is often described as the perfect place for people that love the hippy era. For me, a former hippy and avid roller-blader, it was heaven; the best people-watching spot ever. You'd see an eclectic mix of crazy characters from dreadlocked men on skates playing guitar, to the flower-power brigade wandering around in crocheted miniskirts giving daisies to strangers. Eccentricities are alive and well here.

In the state of California you can only get state-funded welfare benefits for two years; it's why there are so many homeless people. I even saw some homeless men on Venice Beach playing a grand piano during the day, then sleeping under it at night. Because there's not much rain there it was still in tune, even though it was sun-damaged and faded.

I chose to do a bus tour, one that included Compton just south of downtown Los Angeles, the focus of rap songs and riots — including the great uprising triggered in 1992 by the beating of the taxi driver Rodney King by four white cops with batons, in what should have been a fairly routine traffic-stop in the suburb of Lake View Terrace some forty kilometres to the northwest (which also tells you how big and sprawling Los Angeles is).

Footage of the violence, all twelve minutes of it, was sent to a local TV station showing the world that the police's poor treatment of minorities wasn't just something that happened during segregation in the 1950s. It was true that King had been pulled over after a chase, and had been drunk and obnoxious. For that reason the police officers were acquitted of using excessive force.

Still, even the then US President George H. W. Bush said that, in company with some civil rights leaders he was meeting with, he had been "stunned . . . as were my wife Barbara and the kids" by the contrast between the unprofessional conduct shown in the video and the acquittal of the officers, who are supposed to be trained to deal with every kind of situation.

If you watch the video it's hard to believe that lying on the concrete being almost beaten to death by four cops (while another four stand by watching) wasn't anything less than excessive force, the product of a double standard. After all, nothing like that ever happened to Mel Gibson when he was pulled over in a drunk and obnoxious state more recently, nor would it have likely happened back then. But then he is Mel Gibson — and not just some anonymous black guy in 1992.

And so, racial tensions in the city erupted. During the 1992 Los Angeles Riots more than 50 people were killed, over 2,000 were injured and around $1.1 billion worth of damage was caused through looting and arson.

But as informative and moving as that bus tour was, public buses were a different situation. Public transport at that time was dreadful in Los Angeles. The buses were so run-down and stinky that when it was hot and smoggy outside, it was even hotter and smoggier inside. (I hear LA public transport is a lot better now.) So, I hired a car. Learning to drive on the other side of the road — and of the car — took some getting used to. But I got the hang of it. So much so, I drove to Vegas.

LAS VEGAS

The four to five hour road trip north of Los Angeles to Nevada is stunning: flat expansive deserts, craggy pink and red mountain ranges and long straight roads — so different to New Zealand's windy paths through the country. Even though the Mojave Desert looks completely different to New Zealand I noticed one similarity, which is that it has the same volatile weather as Auckland. One minute there's a thunderstorm and the next the sky clears and the sun burns down. Five minutes later my windscreen wipers are on again. I never expected to see four seasons in one hour in my first American desert.

It's no wonder I got a little lost and confused. So confused I ended up on the wrong side of the road and a policewoman saw me. As she was writing out a ticket a motorcycle gang appeared out of nowhere, about six heavy men with ZZ Top-style beards. They started hassling the cop, telling her to cancel the ticket. Being the only females we both felt threatened. To defuse the situation I started telling the bikers that I didn't mind paying the ticket because it was my first one in America! Eventually they left, but being in the middle of nowhere with a gang intimidating a female cop was something I'm not keen to repeat.

The building of the Hoover Dam and the legalisation of gambling in 1931 turned Vegas from a nondescript desert town into a bustling hub for engineers and construction workers, eventually expanding into the party city it's become today.

Vegas doesn't have any hostels because the hotels are so cheap — I was able to get a comfortable room for $15 a night. Hoteliers make their money in Vegas from the gambling floor, which brings in many billions of dollars a year. It's not surprising that six of the world's biggest hotels are in Vegas.

I made a lifelong friend in Vegas — James. A short Irish man whose weight fluctuated between extreme-sport super-fit and chubby, James had just broken up with his girlfriend and was mending his broken heart in Sin City. Women loved him: they were always throwing themselves at him but he was too lost to welcome any of their advances.

We drove to the Grand Canyon together and nothing prepared us for the intensely moving spectacle of seeing it for the first time. It was a photographer's dream; an immense red-rocked gorge with crystal blue water running through it. It was truly breath-taking.

Driving back to Vegas as the sun was setting was incredible. There is something about desert dust that makes the sunsets even more magical than they usually are: it seems to amplify the red and orange colours.

One day we hired a red vintage corvette and drove to the iconic Flamingo Hotel and Casino, built by infamous mobster Bugsy Siegel, one of the first casinos to be built in Vegas and still running today. He named it after his girlfriend at the time, Virginia Hill, a dancer known as the Flamingo because of her long red hair and even longer legs.

Apparently, the Presidential Suite there has a secret ladder and tunnel system down into the underground garage so Bugsy and his mates could escape undetected if necessary. It's one of the most famous landmarks in Vegas: Elvis Presley, Frank Sinatra, Dean Martin and Sammy Davis Jr all performed or filmed movies there.

Vegas is busy. And hot. We wanted to go somewhere cooler and calmer, and decided to head to San Francisco.

I stayed with a friend's daughter there, a cat-loving woman called Angelica. She told me that cat-ownership laws there are really strict. You have to keep their claws clipped to prevent them killing local bird life and you have to control where they go, much like dogs in New Zealand. Most cats are kept indoors: if you've ever had one you know that they're wanderers.

Angelica welcomed me to her city. She put on special dinners and lunches with her good friends: her hospitality was amazing. She showed me around the markets and took me to handfuls of jazz clubs. Even though I'd come here to escape the heat of Vegas it was still sunny. So sunny, that my lips got badly burnt. Walking around with sore-blistered lips is never a good look.

Angelica took me to Napa Valley, the district known for its rolling hills and vineyards, and it didn't disappoint. I never realised that California produced such beautiful wines. We were there on the Fourth of July, America's Independence Day, and I got caught up in the patriotic excitement. Every business and vineyard was flying the flag and it gave me a completely different view of what America was like, in contrast to my pre-conceived political reservations. The sense of patriotism is beautiful: it's so unlike New Zealand.

As much as I loved San Francisco I found the number of oil rigs off the coastline disconcerting. I hope that never happens to New Zealand.

James left San Fran to head back to Ireland and I flew to New Orleans.

NEW ORLEANS

Visiting the birthplace of Jazz was always going to be memorable for me. I love Jazz. And New Orleans didn't disappoint.

It's an incredible blend of French colonial, Spanish and Creole architecture with a delicious dollop of African culture thrown in. The diversity was surprising and inspiring. I was annoyed that it had taken me so long to go to the United States — I'd allowed myself to be indoctrinated to dislike an entire nation based on their nuclear stance. I was delighted that my views had changed.

I was on a tight budget so I stayed in a cheap hostel for 7 nights. It's a thriving city: full of parties, amazing food and festivals, most famously the annual Mardi Gras.

I decided not to drink while I was there because I didn't want to be part of the binge-drinking culture that seemed to permeate the city. And I'm glad I didn't, and kept my wits about me. There were some nutters in the hostel. An Australian woman Karen had a scam going. She'd accuse other guests of theft and was making weekly insurance claims for "lost" items. She also slept with half the hostel.

I learnt about Voodoo in the hostel. A guest I met carried around a voodoo doll and said that whenever she was angry with someone she'd stick a pin in it, and bad things would happen. She believed in the power of it, so I made sure to stay on her good side. Even though voodoo originated in Haiti, it became popular in New Orleans in the 1800s because of Marie Laveau, known as the Voodoo Queen. She had around 12,000 followers of all races, and even today her graveyard is a big tourist attraction.

The name on my passport is Mary Jane, yet I had recently found out that the name on my baptism certificate is actually Jennie. Mum and Dad must have changed their minds somewhere along the way from birth to baptism. Anyway it was great because in New Orleans it is very common to have two names as one. Everyone called me Mary Jane and didn't try to shorten it to just Mary or Jane. It was very normal there.

Bourbon Street is the heart of New Orleans and I was lucky enough to see the legendary jazz trumpeter Dizzy Gillespie perform in a tiny, smoky, fifty-seat venue. He was in his seventies at the time but he played like a thirty year-old. I love live music but seeing him perform was unlike anything I'd ever seen. He's a masterful musician; his cheeks puff up like a chipmunk as he blows his horn. It was amazing! The following night I ended up at a smoke-free jazz venue watching a ninety-five year old musician head to the stage with a walking stick in one hand and a trumpet in the other.

The House of Blues was another highlight — they're a socially responsible venue that feeds the homeless and supports young and local musicians. The stage has a box of Mississippi mud underneath it so that everyone who plays can be grounded to the roots and the spirit of the area. The Creole-inspired menu and music there was incredible: if you're ever in New Orleans, go there. The atmosphere of the room alone will feed your soul.

New Orleans is such a blend of cultures and friendliness mixed with steel string guitars and soaring temperatures. After visiting here I could see similarities between popular musicians: both Sheryl Crow and the Red Hot Chilli Peppers both have that swampy sound.

MEMPHIS, TENNESSEE

Memphis is the artistic birthplace of notable musicians like Aretha Franklin, Isaac Hayes, Al Green, Jerry Lee Lewis and Otis Redding. But its most famous export is The King, Elvis Presley, who started his music career as a teenager there in1954.

His wife Priscilla was only fourteen when they met, but even though they were holidaying together at the age of seventeen, she says in her bestselling autobiography *Elvis and Me* that they didn't have sex until her wedding night, when she was twenty-two.

I love Elvis's lyrics. I had a good look around Graceland. I saw the batik-style room with the black piano where Elvis wrote his music, the pink Cadillac, and all other memorabilia.

NEW YORK, NEW YORK

I don't like late flights into a city. By the time I land and bus into the destination I'm exhausted. But arriving in New York was surprisingly pleasurable, even though it was midnight.

The hostel I'd arranged to stay at was run by a charming Irish man who picked me up at the bus stop. I wasn't expecting New Yorkers to be so accommodating (again another example of my own preconceptions). He told me he could get me a 'green card' for around $100 USD that would give me the right to live and work there. He had a side-business counterfeiting them. When I said no he offered me a job with a female-only furniture moving company. I was just there to travel around, not live and work there, so I declined that too.

He wasn't the only interesting person I met at the hostel. I became hostel-buddies with a struggling twenty-one year-old rapper who was always chasing Swedish girls. He was pretty sure he was going to make it big one day and, sure enough, seven years later in 2003 I started reading reports of a rapper who'd been shot nine times hitting the top of the charts around the world. His name was 50 Cent.

* * *

I'd always admired President Franklin D. Roosevelt's wife Eleanor: she was a powerhouse of a woman and an activist committed to civil rights, women's issues, abolishing child labour and raising the minimum wage. She helped shape New York when her husband was Governor, and the United States of America when he became President.

Being in New York for the first time was overwhelming. Seeing all the iconic buildings we've come to know through movies and television is incredible. And I'm glad I got to experience the city before the terrorist attacks in 2001. I loved going through Times Square in midtown Manhattan. I imagined seeing Woody Allen wandering around, because all of his films were set there. I'd actually seen all of his films and was a huge fan until he married his stepdaughter.

The Statue of Liberty moved me. I was impressed by the philosophy of America's independence from the United Kingdom and the commitment to freedom, progress, and a rough if obviously imperfect kind of equality.

The Empire State building shocked me. Mostly because I was robbed while staring up at it!

Two men unclipped my money belt and raced off with everything — my credit cards and money. I was glad I'd left my passport in the hostel that day! But then being robbed did mean I got to experience the NYPD. I'd seen them on TV and read about them in many books, but walking into the station and meeting actual officers was beyond exciting. And they were happy to meet a rare Kiwi! I sorted out the credit cards on the spot (they were so helpful), but even though it was a pain it resulted in a truly authentic New York experience: one you can't pay for, unless you consider the lost funds as payment.

The Guggenheim Museum made me fall in and out of love with Picasso in one visit. Seeing so many of his works of art in person blew my mind. But the section of the museum that showed twelve of his paintings all in a row showing his former wife and mistresses in various stages of despair repulsed me. I thought it was sick to depict the women in his life as emotionally-crippled tortured souls. I turned off him for life.

1996 was the height of public awareness and media reports of the AIDS epidemic. I even saw a musical about it on Broadway. *Rent* was the story of a group of poor artists and musicians, some of which were HIV-positive, trying to make a living in New York's East Village, which had been a creative but impoverished community in the 1980s. *Rent* was a very successful musical: its 12-year run on Broadway netted more than $280 million. Sadly, its creator, Jonathan Larson, had died of a ruptured blood vessel on the day of the first performance: but at least he saw it accepted for production.

The porn industry in New York was blossoming; everyone in the hostel was watching porn around the clock and it made me uncomfortable, especially as so many people were dying of AIDS.

* * *

I loved America (and I wasn't expecting to). I learned so much about the people and the places I'd been. It was interesting to see how different it was to New Zealand and how inaccurately it had been portrayed in the media. I know now that the political appearance of a country does not reflect its people.

But it was time to leave. And Ireland was a-calling.

CHAPTER TEN
Hitchhiking and Irish Buddhism

I'D made plans to stay in the western Irish city of Limerick, a town founded by Vikings in the eighth century, with friends I'd met in Bali several years earlier.

Ina and John were opposites; she was a strong-willed German lady and he was a laid-back Irish lad. She'd moved to Ireland because she preferred the slow backwards pace of life there, unlike the modern industrialised nature of life in Germany.

Their farmhouse was beautiful: they lived on John's family's dairy farm, although in terms of New Zealand farming it wasn't much to speak of. John had forty cows. Most farms in New Zealand have more than ten times that! He laughed when I told him his farm was tiny. His farm was also surrounded by ancient peat forests. Because a lot of natural forest was cut down in the fourteenth century the government was encouraging and paying for farmers to rebuild the natural landscape. John's farm also had a tourist attraction on it. Apparently the Virgin Mary appeared there in the 1940s, so every year hundreds of pilgrims came to pay their respects.

John and Ina lived there with his mother and aunt. It is not uncommon in Irish families to take in elderly relatives and John was determined to look after his mother and aunt in their golden years.

They took me along to an IRA fundraiser, which was interesting, and John jokingly told everyone that he and I were getting married just so he

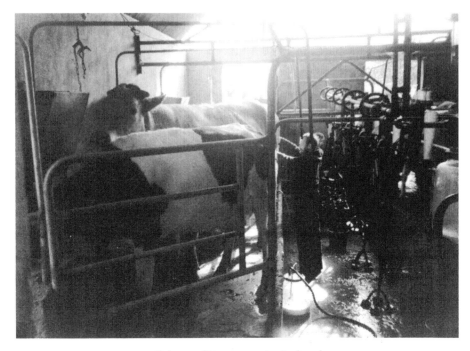

John milking cows in Ireland

could see my reaction when the engagement 'tradition' started. Everyone in the pub kissed me. I was not amused.

Even though he'd joked we were getting married, Ina and John got engaged for real while I was staying with them, and we had a big party to celebrate. Engagement parties are very different events in Ireland; they're usually in a café/restaurant and guests pay for their own food. Even though the alcohol was supplied and paid for by Ina and John it wasn't a big boozy affair like you'd expect in New Zealand. It was civilised.

They took me to *Passahhdi*, a Buddhist retreat in the Beara Peninsula just outside a place called Adrigole.

I've always felt an affinity to Buddhism; there's gentleness to their worship that impresses me. About an hour into our first lesson, a former Catholic priest was talking about heaven and hell and I burst out laughing. I couldn't see the relevance of heaven and hell to *Buddhism*! Even though I was embarrassing Ina and John, I just couldn't stop giggling.

* * *

Ireland has a long and often tragic history: from Neolithic times through various rebellions against English and British rule, the devastating Potato Famine in the mid-1800s and the Irish Civil War in the 1920s, through to Troubles in Northern Ireland in more recent decades and the financial upheavals of the present day.

The Potato Famine, perhaps the most traumatic episode in a series of traumas, was named after the humble root vegetable because nearly half of the population relied on it for food. Around a million people died after disease wiped out their crops and another million emigrated – mostly to America and Australia. The famine thus removed about a quarter of the country's population of eight million, which then continued to steadily decline to about four million by the early 1900s. Meanwhile the population of Great Britain and the rest of Europe leaped ahead by leaps and bounds. The record of British rule in Ireland really was a disaster.

To look out over Ireland with its rolling glossy green hills, it's hard to believe that a nation of such laid-back people come from such a turbulent and violent history. But then you're never far from reminders. There are crosses everywhere. Plonked down in the middle of fields; everywhere you look you see white Gaelic crosses and ancient tombstones.

After a wonderful time staying with my dear friends I decided to hitchhike around the country. I met a man who had travelled to New

Zealand representing the Irish Agricultural Minister. He told me that the Canterbury Plains reminded him so much of Ireland he used pictures of them in promotional brochures advertising Ireland! I hope it was a joke.

I hitchhiked northwest to the Aran Islands where I saw a peculiar blend of arctic, Mediterranean and alpine plants all growing in the same place. Apparently they have some unusual soil and the winds blow in all directions bringing with it different seeds onto the islands.

The Aran Island's claim to fame is having the smallest church in the world. *Teampall Bheanáin* is an 11th century stone building that measures 3.2 by 2.1 metres. It's also now the home of many quirky annual sell-out events, like the Red Bull Cliff Diving Competition and the Father Ted Festival (because the TV show set in fictional Craggy Island was filmed there).

There's a curious vegetable growing method here. Because most of the island is rock they have to put seaweed on top of the rocks to turn it into pasture. They call the term "lazy bed" and it's often used to grow potatoes. Apparently seaweed is a great fertiliser and it's a plentiful free resource.

Even though Ireland's national flower is the shamrock, the most prolific flower is *furze*. The bright yellow blooms light up the landscape, but don't plan on skipping through fields of flowers; the prickly thorny leaves will leave you in shreds. In New Zealand furze is known as gorse and we're always trying to get rid of it, but in Ireland the flowers are used in salads, boiled down for natural remedies or turned into gorse flower wine, which my mother also used to make.

I'd always wanted to see Van Morrison live, but to see him play in front of an Irish audience at the one-day Millstreet Music Fair in Cork was incredible.

The venue was small by outdoor concert standards, and the crowd of around five thousand couldn't have been more enthusiastic or appreciated. The Irish *love* Irish performers: especially ones with such recognisable songs. I also saw Shane MacGowan from the Pogues; the Corrs; and the Irish version of the Von Trapps, the Kelly Family, who have sold over twenty million albums since the early 1980s.

Although my time in Ireland was wonderful; it was time to leave. And this time, instead of hitchhiking around, I was using a slightly more reliable mode of transport: a bus.

CHAPTER ELEVEN
Europe by Bus

Around four million people a year use Eurolines: an inexpensive inter-country hop-on-hop off intercity coach network. I paid around $850 for a ticket that gave me access to six hundred destinations in thirty-six countries.

Not only was I excited about visiting so many different countries; I was excited to find out what sort of people would be travelling on the bus.

I headed down from Ireland to Paris, and then jumped off to visit the Louvre with an Australian girl Belinda I'd met on-board. Belinda became my travelling companion. Belinda was twenty, on a gap year and was from Melbourne. She was slim, blonde and drank little, compared to the others on the bus. She appreciated art culture and the old buildings and paintings. Most of the other passengers were heading to Oktoberfest, the annual German beer festival — personally, I couldn't think of anything worse.

The Louvre is one of my favourite places and it seems like I'm not alone; it's the second-most visited museum in the world. With nearly thirty-five thousand objects and artworks it's also the biggest art museum in the world.

We caught the high speed TGV train down to Versailles and even though I'd been to the Palace before with Niels, I'd never visited the Royal Opera House. It didn't disappoint.

Built in the 1770s to celebrate the marriage of Louis XVI to Marie Antoinette, it was used only for royal ceremonies and special occasions.

The Eurolines Network: main routes and centres (Eurolines)

Apparently it was too expensive to stage productions there if it wasn't for a major event. It has a stunning baroque interior; the soft blue, gold and cream-coloured lavishness makes you feel like you're standing inside an expensive, ornate music box.

GERMANY

I'll never forget the shop window displays in Frankfurt. Every single window was dressed to perfection; the bakeries, markets and butchers all had individual scenes that were like works of art. The fishmonger's was incredible: steaks from each fish hanging around a miniature fishing scene and each fish head was neatly arranged on slabs of stone. Even the kitchen shop joined in; they'd created tin-robot creatures out of pots and pans. It was a very inventive and unique way to sell products.

A short hour-long ride south of Frankfurt was Heidelberg, the famous university town. Heidelberg is a beautiful place, filled with dreamy romantic baroque-styled buildings — it's like being in a Disney film.

The six hour journey to Berlin was a pleasant enough trip, but landing in the capital was difficult. To be in a city with such a turbulent past troubled me. I suppose you can never really prepare yourself to be in a place with such recent negative history. The Berlin Wall was built to cut the Soviet-occupied East Germany off from West Germany. Built in 1961, it symbolised hatred and divided communities and families. If you were seen trying to escape from the East to the West you were shot at, and thrown in prison if caught. Many Germans who were trapped in the East fled through a loophole to Austria and Hungary in the last days of the Wall in autumn 1989, eventually helping to dilute the power of the Soviet Union as well. The Soviet Union itself ceased to exist on Christmas Day 1991, just two years after the opening of the Wall. There are still parts of the Wall on display in Berlin; it was haunting.

The Checkpoint Charlie museum is grim. One image stood out for me; a photo of a little blonde girl trying to get through the wire fence, while her former neighbours watched. To stand where the Nazis burnt books gave me chills, as well. Denying people literature was just one of the ways to control and subdue free-thinking.

As much as I loved parts of Germany, Berlin disturbed me.

ITALY

I love Italy. The art, the architecture, the historical churches, the people — it's a place that inspires and relaxes me.

Rome is one of the best cities to wander about in. Every street has famous landmarks or an interesting past.

I'd always wanted to go to the Vatican City. Having been raised a Roman Catholic meant that I had a lifelong fascination with Rome and the Vatican. Seeing the baroque style of art and architecture in person was better than I could ever have expected.

What surprised me the most, though, was how much classical architecture from two thousand years ago, originally of Greek inspiration, has survived. In fact, there seemed to be more classical architecture in Rome than in Greece!

* * *

While there, I found a postcard to send to my dear friend Mark Allen in New Zealand. A political activist who worked for the Unemployed Rights Centre in Auckland, Mark was a self-taught legal advocate who defended people's rights.

The postcard that was never sent. I signed it Arohanui, 'big love' in Māori

I hadn't spoken to Mark in a while and had forgotten his address so called a mutual buddy to find his contact details. Tragically, he had died suddenly of a heart attack that morning: the day I was going to send him a postcard! I wish I had sent it earlier — don't let such time go by.

Mark's death dampened my Vatican visit; it was difficult to fully enjoy the splendour of the Sistine Chapel while devastated about losing my friend so unexpectedly.

* * *

But, as incredible as Rome was, it didn't compare to the beauty of Venice.

Venice was my favourite stop of my entire European trip. I've never seen so many gold details, eagles, and phoenixes before!

The Gallerie dell' Accademia on the south bank of the Grand Canal blew me away. It was one of the first museums in the world to specialise in restoration, and as they've been committed to studying how best to renovate and refurbish ancient works of art since 1777, they're experts.

With the world's best collection of Venetian art from the fourteenth to the eighteenth century, the Gallerie dell'Accademia is an art-lovers dream. The rich colours instantly took my breath away, with many works featuring dramatic depictions of religious scenes from the Last Supper to Mary's coronation. After a month in Italy, it was time to head west.

Venice

SPAIN

I hopped off in Valencia, the third largest city in Spain (after Madrid and Barcelona) and headed west to the small cultural hotspot of Toledo.

Toledo has a rich history. Jews, Christians and Muslims have lived here together peacefully for over a thousand years, giving it the nickname, "The City of Three Cultures." Wandering around the city transports you to another time: old buildings, Roman roads and olive trees makes you feel like you're in a pre-medieval era.

A four-hour drive south, and I'm in Granada, at the bottom of the stunning Sierra Nevada Mountain range – my favourite place in Spain. There are fewer tourists here, and it is home to an incredible Arabic palace and fortress called the Alhambra. Originally completed in 889AD, the

Alhambra was converted into a royal residence in 1333. Decorated with neutral-coloured geometrical and ornately carved symmetrical patterns, it's an amazing piece of Islamic architecture set in lush gardens.

There is music everywhere in Granada. One of my most vivid memories was stumbling across a street flamenco performance. It was the first time I'd heard true flamenco. Witnessing the passionate dancing and hearing the guttural tones of the singer — she sang from her stomach not just her mouth — made my jaw drop.

Belinda and I danced and sang along even though I didn't know the words, but I was stoned and tipsy and partying with gypsies until five in the morning.

After a big sleep-in I headed south to Algeciras to catch the ferry to Morocco.

MOROCCO

The ferries to Morocco are fast. And cheap. Belinda and I met a few people on-board, and we all decided we would explore Morocco together.

We landed in the port of Tangier, which in the 1950s was a popular holiday destination for Europeans. Tangier is a melting pot of many different ethnicities: Arabic, Berber, French and nomadic tribes who still live in the Sahara Desert. There are many languages here. Berber and Moroccan Arabic are the main ones made use of by local people. But French, the language of the former French colonisers, is used on signs and in administration, as is more formal or classical Arabic. Many Moroccans also speak Spanish due to past Spanish colonialism; and English is widely understood in tourist areas as well.

Tangier unsettled me: I almost instantly had an experience I'd rather

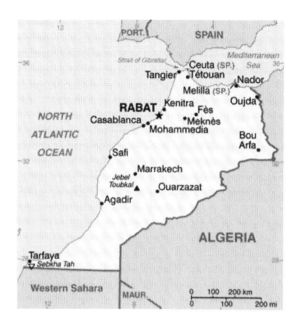

forget. We were wandering around the city when I was confronted by a man with a large knife demanding money. But none of us had any cash to give him (we were all travelling on a budget) so I yelled at him to "Go get a job!" Which was possibly a little insensitive in view of the likely rate of unemployment locally. He argued with me for a while but I just kept shouting that I'd call the police. He didn't seem to understand exactly what I was saying but soon backed off. I was shaken by the experience. I decided to get out of Tangier and head south.

We headed to Essaouira, a small historical fortress town on the Atlantic Coast in Morocco. It felt like a French town, and I later discovered that much of the fortification had been built by French engineers in the eighteenth century, the same ones that had built similarly fortified ports on the coast of France. Even though Essaouira is a coastal town, the sand blows in pretty hard from the desert, so it's not a relaxing beach area.

Eassaouira is most famous for being the supposed inspiration behind Jimi Hendrix's *Castles Made of Sand* — although there's some debate whether it's just an urban myth. Hendrix did visit in 1969, but the song he supposedly wrote after seeing the half-buried Bordj El Berod fortress watchtower was actually released two years before his visit! Locals justify it by saying he came here in secret several years earlier. Regardless, there's a café there called Café Jimi Hendrix and many famous musicians came to Essaouira in the 1960s and 1970s: The Rolling Stones, Frank Zappa, Maria Callas, Bob Marley and Paul Simon.

We stayed there for a week, and spent most of our time trying to avoid seven and eight year-old boys trying to sell us hash!

*Essaouira, where Jimi is unreliably purported
to have written* Castles Made of Sand

We moved on to Marrakesh, a visually rich city. The deep hues of spices and jewel-toned fabric stalls in the market offset the faded pink buildings and the dusty desert landscape. But it's not just the colours that contradict each other: there's a stark contrast between the poor and the rich. The tourists have their own police, there to assist in English if they need any help.

Being in an Islamic country was quite a culture shock for me. Women aren't allowed in cafes and are still segregated from men in public outside the busy tourist areas. It's normal for men to hold hands and be affectionate with each other here, but in New Zealand it's less common and generally only if you're homosexual. But of course homosexuality is frowned upon in Islamic countries, which I find ridiculous.

We dressed carefully in Morocco. I wore long skirts and dresses with tops that covered my arms. But there were still lots of Europeans around that wore bikinis and miniskirts in public and didn't give a damn. I thought it was a bit rude: dressing modestly showed respect for the culture. Of course, if I was near the water I'd wear togs, but something more modest outside the pool area. The one thing I noticed about the heat was that even though it's scorching hot in Morocco, the sun isn't as harsh as in New Zealand. I didn't get sunburnt here (and I don't recall using sunscreen!)

Again, we had a scary incident. Belinda and I were walking around the outskirts of the city when a stranger came up and punched me in the breast. I was shocked. And it hurt. It was completely unprovoked, we were both fully covered and we weren't with any men. He ran away after I screamed at him. It was such a random act of violence that I struggled to make sense of it. But I didn't let it ruin my trip; almost every other person I'd met in Morocco was helpful and super-friendly.

In fact they were so friendly Belinda and I were invited to the Sahara

Desert to eat dinner with some nomadic Berber people. It's apparently a sign of great honour to be asked (and very disrespectful to decline) so of course we went.

The trip down to the desert from Marrakesh was insane: I felt like I was on another planet. Giant red mountains, lush green fields, dusty orange plains, deserted North African villages and donkeys everywhere carrying firewood; it was amazing. And then we saw the camels and the rising golden dunes of the Sahara.

The shepherds slow-cooked us deliciously-spiced lamb tagine with couscous in handmade clay pots on Moroccan fire pits, the fragrant smells tantalising our tastebuds. The nomads smoked weed and we talked, laughed and shared stories from our home countries. I had a short fling with a Berber Rastafarian — that's what holidays are for right?

It was time to leave Morocco and head back to see friends in France.

CHAPTER TWELVE
Corsica

AFTER a few days in Marseille eating beautiful food with strong Arabic and Moroccan influences, Belinda and I decided to head to Corsica to stay with some old friends of mine from *Elf-Chine*, the Chinese junk.

Even though Corsica has been under France's rule for two centuries, it still feels like it's a separate country: the food, the languages (French and Corsican) and the culture.

The birthplace of Napoleon is beautiful: most of the villages were built on top of mountains with sweeping views over the turquoise Mediterranean waters, because it gave the people a natural advantage over invading armies.

And there were many. Corsica changed hands constantly between the Greeks, Romans, Byzantines, Italians, French, British and Germans, not to mention a brief period of self-rule.

I adored the Corsican language (Corse); it sounds like a bird singing. Even though it sounds Spanish with lots of soft melodic vowel sounds, it's actually very similar to Italian. The way Italian and French have combined to make a new language was just beautiful.

My friend Claude had bought a property here in the 1970s. It was basically a shed that housed surfboards. Claude's friend, Bernard had a large family home there: he'd grown up on the island. Belinda and I each had our own room with beautiful shuttered windows. It was a nice change to have some space and privacy. I couldn't remember the last time I'd not shared a room or dorm with somebody.

We didn't have a car on the island, so we just hitchhiked everywhere and it was safe, apart from one time. Two dodgy shepherds picked us up and immediately turned off the main road to take us down some side roads to have their way with us. I yelled at them in French that I knew what they were doing and they stopped and let us out in the middle of nowhere. It was terrifying, but I'd never been so glad to be stranded.

Bernard told us not to go walking on Sundays because that's the day everyone goes hunting. Belinda and I thought he was exaggerating, so we headed off on a small bush walk, but we didn't last long. Sure enough, every man and his dog on the island was out with a gun. Off to get some fresh meat for Sunday dinner. We turned around and headed back to the house; I didn't fancy ending up as a meal.

And speaking of meals; on Corsica they're intense: rich French sauces — plenty of duck, goose and game, and four-course meals every night. And with nine wine regions on the island there's no shortage of world-class beverages. Plus everyone drinks goat's milk instead of cow's milk. I'm not sure I'd ever really drunk it before — definitely not in New Zealand — but the rich salty flavour agreed with me. But not with my waistline; the food and wine and milk made me fat. And I'd only been there two weeks!

It was time to leave. I was overweight and needed to do some exercise. We ferried to Nice and bussed to Grasse, the perfume capital of the world, to do some rock climbing. But it wasn't for me. I don't like the feeling of being tied up.

Free-climbing with a pack, yes. Heights and ropes limiting my movement? No thanks. It made me anxious.

So, it wasn't a long stay in the south of France. Vienna was calling my name.

CHAPTER THIRTEEN
Back on the Bus

V IENNA, the capital of Austria, is a mix of over-the-top historical buildings and an ultra-modern buzzing nightlife. Even though Austria looks like a wealthy country due to its lavish architecture it was relatively cheap then, so it was perfect for travellers on a budget. Vienna was so clean — I don't think I saw a single piece of litter or graffiti anywhere. And I was looking out for it.

I saw one of my favourite pieces of art in Vienna, in the Österreichische Galerie Belvedere Museum. Austrian artist Gustav Klimt made a number of paintings during his 'gold period' where he combined gold leaf and paint to create shimmering works of art. *The Kiss* is his most popular piece and you can clearly see the Turkish influences in his design; the painting looks like it's made from hundreds of tiny mosaic fragments.

After a short stay in the capital we headed to Innsbruck to get a sense of how people lived outside the main centres. I'm so glad we did.

Candy-coloured five-storey buildings built against the backdrop of the Karwendel Alps, with villagers working in the fields with hand tools. I felt like we'd gone back in time.

After only a few days in Austria my feet were itchy. And I was hungry for more adventures.

We jumped back on the coach and headed southeast for three hours to the Hungarian capital of Budapest, and found a super-budget hostel within minutes of landing. For only five New Zealand dollars a night we had a shared dorm room and an evening meal. But the meal was odd: cheap but not cheerful. It was a goulash with a piece of fatty yellow chewy slimy meat floating on the top. I'd never tasted anything like it (and I'm pretty sure it was horse meat).

We met a crazy Australian man called Rod there. He'd sold his house and was spending all his money on drinking. And bizarrely I ran into Karen, the woman from New Orleans who was claiming insurance on everything and blaming other travellers for theft. We avoided them both.

Budapest had a touch of sadness. A lot of the public art work and monuments were created during the Soviet rule after World War II and, even though Communist rule had ended years earlier, you could still see the strong Soviet influence everywhere.

Beauty spas in Budapest are something else. We went to the Arab baths and were scrubbed down from head to toe until all the black gunk came out of our pores. I was amazed that my skin had so many impurities, not for long though!

Another coach ride for four hours northward, and we were in Slovakia, the less developed and industrialised half of the recently broken-up Czechoslovakia, which had divided in two in 1993 in a completely peaceful manner, in stark contrast to Yugoslavia which was also breaking up at around that time.

Slovakia was filled with castles and dramatic scenery of mountaintop villages, soaring peaks and wooded forests, but at the same time it was less touristy than other places in Europe we'd visited. Slovakia in those immediately post-Communist days wasn't geared up for visitors. Hostels and venues weren't really sure how to handle tourists; they almost seemed a little surprised by foreigners. But they were still lovely people to be around even if, or perhaps because, they didn't 'get' tourism.

We didn't stay long, though.

Seven hours northwest on the coach and we were in Prague in the Czech Republic, the other half of the former Czechoslovakia. What a country! Every single person I know that's been to Prague has raved about it. And I could understand why. It's a grand city filled with beautifully preserved cobblestone roads, castles, colourful baroque buildings and gothic architecture, but with a modern vibrancy and buzz that catches you by surprise. It's the fifth most visited European city and one of the cheapest spots to visit on the continent.

Prague is magnificent. I loved my time there. Even though it was short, I'll definitely go back again one day.

We had time for one more stop; Amsterdam. So, we hopped back on and travelled ten hours northwest to the heart of the Netherlands.

I'd always dreamt of being able to legally smoke weed in a bar, in public, so Amsterdam gave me a sense of freedom. But this trip was riddled with awkwardness. An Irish couple on the coach were drunk and abusive to each other, and the general vibe at the hostel was annoying. I didn't want to hang out with assholes, let alone stoned assholes. I said my goodbyes to Belinda — she'd been a wonderful travel buddy — and headed back to London so I could return to New Zealand.

CHAPTER FOURTEEN

Time to Settle Down in New Zealand, for a Minute

AFTER so many adventures I decided it was time to stay in New Zealand and build a career, so I enrolled in a post-graduate diploma in secondary teaching. Little did I know I was in for a rude awakening.

The course was full of complex and interesting issues. One of the training sessions was about learning to deal with a female student that wanted to be a male. Now in 1997 there was very little knowledge or acceptance of cross-gender children or adults. I remember thinking that it wasn't a serious issue because it wouldn't be very common. But in reality it's a pressing issue in our society and all over the world.

I went on several placements where you get to teach in schools with varying age groups. Sadly, I was part-way through my course when I realised that I couldn't teach in my favourite subject, history, because there weren't enough students interested in learning about it.

Such a shame. In fact, why should history be optional? Why should the choice to study history be left up to students who have not yet lived through very much of it?

I was placed in Auckland's Mt Albert Boys Grammar, now co-ed and called Mt Albert Grammar: one of the largest schools in the country. I was teaching social studies and was stunned to discover that the majority of my class of Polynesian and Māori children didn't know their whakapapa, their ancestral heritage. Instead of using the school's textbooks to teach them about their heritage, I started playing music by New Zealand rapper Savage to inspire them to ask around at home about their families and backgrounds.

The kids loved it. They started writing their own raps and many of them came back to school with newly discovered information about their ancestry. I was happy that I'd been able to encourage a discussion around paternal lineage. The school was not happy with this exercise: rap music wasn't as well received in mainstream society then (like hip hop is now) so I suspect they thought I was too much of a maverick.

At Lynfield College, I'd also arranged for the then Green MP Nándor Tánczos to come and speak to my class, but his visit was vetoed by the school because of his stance on the decriminalisation of marijuana. I told the school to get stuffed; I won't be told what to think and how to act, and I resent the fact that we cannot use drugs for personal use in New Zealand. I hung up pro-pot pamphlets around the staff room. That went down well.

I finally graduated in 1998 along with my friend Claire Duncan, a very clever woman who was already using computer software long before it became a fundamental part of teaching practices. She was ahead of her time.

I started teaching at De La Salle College, a Catholic Boys school in South Auckland. De La Salle was leading a programme to track student literacy and improve performance by keeping student records to improve student performance. Many committed teachers did extracurricular activity to help students. De La Salle is the leading Catholic School in the country now used as an example for other Catholic schools to emulate.

All the same, it was a shock to the system and it opened my eyes to a whole other side of teaching. I started off the job healthy and fit but by the end of my time there I'd gained seven kilograms and was stressed out. The boys here were tough; I was told to get fucked on a daily basis and according to school statistics, a third of the boys in my class had been sexually abused.

Two brothers at De La Salle called me Madonna. I took it as a compliment. I guess they thought my outspoken style of expressing myself reminded them of the ballsy popstar.

The school was big on sporting achievements. A number of former All Blacks and other notable athletes are former alumni. One day I entered the school's hockey team into a local tournament. Unfortunately one of the star first-fifteen rugby players, who also played hockey, fell over and broke his arm. And I was blamed for it! Rugby players are revered in New Zealand, and apparently I shouldn't have encouraged him to play hockey.

As it was a Catholic school I was required to go to mass. And I found that my views often conflicted with those represented by the school. I supported gay rights and had to constantly defend my views to colleagues and students. I told my class one day that as the Anglican Church hadn't banned homosexuality why should the Catholic Church? I believed that God loves everyone so I couldn't understand the hypocrisy.

And then one student tried to kill himself. Apparently he'd had a relationship with a young teacher. What appalled me was that despite the situation being brought to the school's attention the teacher was able to leave without so much as a slap on the wrist. But then that wasn't an uncommon strategy within school environments in that era. The Oscar-winning film *Spotlight* uncovered systemic levels of child abuse in Boston in the United States of America; all of which was deliberately concealed by more powerful members of the clergy, issues common across the world in that era.

I became the spokesperson for the campaign for public transport at the time with my friends Chris Harris and Michael Heath Caldwell. We were committed to finding alternative transportation methods and opposed motorway expansion. Michael was going to stand for the ACT party with Alex Swney (who was later imprisoned for submitting false invoices) and worked hard for a number of community- focused organisations.

It all got too much.

I was investing so much energy trying to improve things at the school and in the community that I was emotionally and physically drained. I was grumpy and sluggish due to the weight I put on from comfort eating. I needed a change. Not from teaching; just from the intense challenges that De La Salle bought.

So, I moved to Papatoetoe High School to take the role of Head of Economics, thinking that no school could be as bad as the previous one. I was wrong. I was surprised that I was given a managerial position so early in my teaching career but soon discovered that it was because no-one else wanted it (the other teachers were dropping like flies from the stress of this environment).

In most schools, it seems the students used emotional blackmail to bully teachers into giving them good grades. Students would regularly accuse teachers of being gay or lesbian and would threaten to tell authorities that they'd been molesting them. It was awful, and I saw several great teachers leave over these unfounded accusations and threats. There was a climate of absolute fear operating here; the students had power over the teachers and there was no way to shift it.

So I left.

I tried another school, but it was more of the same: teachers were not only verbally abused, but there were physical altercations as well. And the school didn't support the teaching staff.

I was becoming very disillusioned with the education system so I took a break to get my head around what had happened. In my first year of teaching I became involved with the PPTA, New Zealand's Post Primary Teachers' Association. I ended up becoming the Treasurer (which wasn't an easy job).

By the end of my tenure at the PPTA, I'd more than balanced the books and had saved the union $27,000. The teachers on the PPTA got laptops which was great. But we disagreed about procedures: I was thought to be too officious about money, not flexible or something.

Even though working for the union was frustrating I do believe they're a necessity. It was the neoliberal agenda that brought in New Zealand's current educational standards and the National Certificate of Achievement (NCEA). It's a competitive approach to learning rather than the previous co-operative approach. However, the vast majority of the NCEA qualification is now internally assessed, not externally assessed as it once was. There are a lot of pros and cons to the new system and it's vastly different from when I was at school.

After all these disappointments I went to heal in the best way possible. With travel.

CHAPTER FIFTEEN

Vietnam

My friend Rose Segedin and I decided to go to Ho Chi Minh City (Saigon) to stay with some pals from the *Elf-Chine*. Mary Budgen lived there with her husband and son for half the year; the rest of the year they stayed in France.

Their house in Vietnam was amazing: four levels, six bedrooms and a live-in maid who cost them only $100 a month. That seems cheap, but it was nearly three times the monthly minimum wage of around $35.

Vietnam was busy, super-friendly and inexpensive. I got an entire silk wardrobe made to measure; beautiful dresses and a corporate wardrobe of skirts, jackets and trousers, all of which fitted perfectly. Everyone in Vietnam seemed to work; from making crafts or running street-food stalls. My favourite place to go to had around thirty different wrapped rice rolls with every filling possible from pork to coconut rat (if you saw the rat climbing up a coconut tree you could ask them to catch it, skin it and cook it for you in a coconut broth!).

We visited the War Remnants museum — the official museum of the Vietnam War — one of the longest and costliest conflicts in history. Around three million people were killed in the two-decade long war between the Communist North and the South and its allies, mainly the United States of America. Eventually the Americans withdrew following mounting pressure back home, and North Vietnam took the reluctant South under its Communist wing.

The exhibitions in the museum were profoundly shocking. Photos of United States of America soldiers abusing the Vietnamese and the effects of Agent Orange, the notorious air-dropped herbicide the Americans used to destroy forest cover. Similar to the herbicides 2,4,5-T and 2,4-D that were widely used by farmers and gardeners in those days, Agent Orange contained toxic impurities that caused all kinds of deformities and illnesses among people and wildlife that were exposed to it. Animals that depended on the forest also starved and died. My visit to the museum still haunts me today. I understand that many of the confronting displays and images have been removed now, but back then, deformed foetuses ranging from four to nine months old in glass jars made me feel physically sick. I had to leave. Heading outdoors to get some fresh air and seeing one of the planes used to drop the toxins left me visibly disturbed.

We headed to the beach to clear our heads (and hearts) and were surprised to see a filthy, plastic-bag littered beach. Rose and I began helping the locals to clear the beach of all the bags; I guess they'd blown in from the city and, as the sand was damp and sticky, they just ended up settling there.

Rose and I hired some motorbikes to go see the Mekong Delta, three hours south of Ho Chi Minh City. The Mekong Delta is a place where the Mekong River empties into the sea. It's a biologically diverse area and an important ecological region of Vietnam. I thought it was a really beautiful and special place; the lush green forest and unspoilt landscape gave it a spiritual quality.

We visited a coconut candy factory, a family-run business that makes candy by hand from all natural ingredients. Nothing is wasted here. Banana lollies are made from banana leaves and even the husks were used to fuel the fires.

The rice paddies were amazing: winding layers of bright green steps throughout the countryside. It couldn't be more different than the sheep-covered rolling hills of New Zealand. I couldn't get over how friendly everyone was. They had plenty to be upset about given their tortured history, but they didn't show it.

We ended up in a small rural town called Huyen and had a French-Vietnamese meal, five courses of incredible fresh flavours — coconut crab, lemongrass-dressed pork salad and desserts — for only $5.

Vietnam was one of my favourite places to visit, despite its tragic past. But it was time to keep on moving: so we headed to China.

CHAPTER SIXTEEN
Oriental Lightning

W E flew from Tan Son Nhat international airport to Hong Kong, where we stayed with a mutual friend. Hong Kong is an assault on the senses; the city literally never sleeps. I thought Vietnam was busy but this was the next level. Even though there it had a similar population to Ho Chi Minh City, Hong Kong was more frenetic.

A European friend of mine showed us around the city and pointed out which live fish in restaurants were safe and not safe to eat. He swore that many of the fish tanks were filled with sewage water. He advised us to never eat seafood in Hong Kong, unless we want food poisoning.

Immediately, I wanted to get out into the hills to get back to nature and hike. I'd heard that nearby there was some of the best tramping in the region, so I organised a day-tour and headed off by myself.

Plover Cover Country Park in the northeast is a serene retreat from the hustle and bustle of the city. The brown grassy hills and slopes reminded me of summer-dried hills in Okura/Long Bay in Auckland. But the rice paddies were a very different feature! I was surprised. And then I was doubly surprised.

As I was hiking a bolt of lightning struck the ground a metre in front of me. I jumped back in shock, wondering whether it had anything to do with an affair I'd been having with a man separated from his wife. It was not something I was proud of either and it had been playing on my mind when I was nearly struck.

CHAPTER SEVENTEEN
The Not So New Caledonia

NOUVELLE Calédonie, known in English as New Caledonia, is a French-administered, French-speaking island territory lying on the Tropic of Capricorn, east of Queensland and north-west of New Zealand.

The largest island in the territory, Grand Terre, is 350 km long, and is the island on which the territory's capital, Nouméa, is located. This is the island that New Zealanders think of when New Caledonia is mentioned, and it is the one Captain Cook named New Caledonia to begin with, as for some reason it reminded him of Scotland.

But today Grande Terre is only one of the islands of the French territory of New Caledonia, which also includes the Îles Loyauté (Loyalty Islands), the Île des Pins (Isle of Pines), the Chesterfield Islands and the Belep Archipelago among others.

In the year 2000, the total population of the territory was only a quarter of a million. That year was also the year of my first visit to New Caledonia — and once more, my sister was travelling with me.

I was still trying to leave my disappointing teaching experience behind. So, I was irritated that the hotel we were staying in was full of noisy, yelling, screaming school children (and teachers) from Australia and New Zealand. Every night they ran up and down the hallways: it was a nightmare.

Maree and I hired a car, and while out exploring we came across a New Zealand grave site with a New Zealand flag flying. This was the Bourail

New Zealand War Cemetery, which includes a monument inscription to seventeen New Zealand Coastwatchers executed by the Japanese on Tarawa in late 1942. Coastwatchers were radio operators employed by the New Zealand Government Post and Telegraph Department, mostly civilians (and thus liable to be treated as spies) who were placed on islands all over the South Pacific Ocean from the sub-Antarctic to the equator to report on southward Japanese shipping and aircraft movements after Pearl Harbour. Many were captured as the Japanese moved south and their treatment varied considerably depending on how strict the local Japanese commander was; the ones commemorated in Bourail had drawn the short straw. In December 1942 the New Zealand Government realised its omission and gave the Coastwatchers military rank.

The unfortunate seventeen New Zealanders commemorated in Bourail had been executed on Tarawa along with a smaller number of Britons and Australians. The Japanese never quite got to New Caledonia. But Bourail was where they were buried as it had been a New Zealand military base in World War II. Bourail had been the headquarters of the Third New Zealand Division which was put on New Caledonia to defend the territory from in-vasion, and was the natural site for a Pacific Theatre war cemetery thereafter.

It was totally unexpected, quite surreal and frightening. We had no idea prior to finding the graves that this was even here, or that Bourail had even existed.

Everybody in New Zealand has a relative who fought against the Germans or the Italians in World War II — or so it seems. Indeed, New Zealanders do mostly think of WWII in terms of granddad's part in the downfall of Rommel, Mussolini, or the German commander in Italy, Albert Kesselring.

Plus, of course, all those New Zealanders who flew in the Battle of Britain and RAF Bomber Command, not to mention the part played by the Royal

New Zealand Navy in the sinking of the *Graf Spee*.

But the fact that New Zealanders were in the Pacific too, both as Coastwatchers and as combatants in some of the battles as well, seems to be forgotten by comparison.

Phil Amos, the Minister of Education in New Zealand's 1972-1975 Labour Government whom I mentioned earlier, flew as a navigator in Royal New Zealand Air Force Grumman Avenger torpedo bombers in the Pacific during World War II. This puts Phil in the same select company as the former US President George H. W. Bush, who piloted the same aircraft for the US Navy in the Pacific. I mean Bush senior of course, not to be confused with George W. Bush.

But due to a rather colonial tendency to over-identify with Britain and its predicament in 1940, or in reality also because most New Zealand casualties by far were incurred in Europe and North Africa, the New Zealanders came to forget about the Pacific War even though it happened in our backyard.

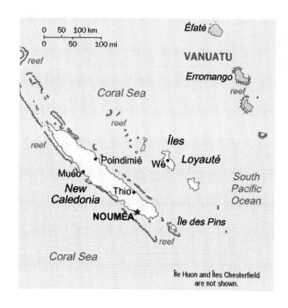

New Zealand was full of US Marines at the time, and major American operations of the Pacific War were planned in Auckland. And yet it was all largely forgotten about as soon as it was over.

The Third New Zealand Division were disparaged as the 'Coconut Bombers': but they would have had more work to do if Japanese forces had made it to New Caledonia.

One unexpectedly positive consequence of a tendency to forget about the Pacific War was that the anti-Japanese and more generally anti-Asian animus that took hold in Australia after World War II was never seen in post-War New Zealand. Japanese-style interior décor came to be seen as the last word in sophistication in post-War New Zealand. Our economic hopes also came to be pinned on closer cooperation with countries like Japan, Indonesia and China, at a time when the average Australian wouldn't have been seen dead driving a Japanese car and had the gravest reservations about the various other sources of the 'yellow peril' as well.

And so, by a strange reverse irony, post-War Australia became more Eurocentric and fearful of its physical position on the globe — every 1960s Australian schoolkid's atlas showing the whole of Asia about to descend on their little heads — even as New Zealand became less focused on a historic colonial Britishness, and to embrace the Pacific and Asia at last.

Getting back to New Caledonia, Maree and I were based in Nouméa, and there were a few things I didn't like about that place. Maree and I went on a cruise celebrating different Pacific Islands. I met a professor from Waikato University in New Zealand who was Melanesian: that is to say from the large islands of the South-Western Pacific, of which Grande Terre is one.

This professor was originally from the Solomon Islands. But the Solomons are close to New Caledonia, and the people are related to the indigenous inhabitants of New Caledonia.

He said that he found it extremely insulting to be in New Caledonia on board a cruise where the entertainment consisted of Tahitian dancers, the Tahitians being a completely different culture from the South-Eastern Pacific, a culture more like that of the New Zealand Māori as it happens.

Tahitians come from an island group whose only connection to New Caledonia is that Tahiti, too, is run by the French. Where was the local Melanesian, that is, South-Western Pacific culture?

I agreed with him. As an academic might say, to have Tahitian entertainment on a cruise through the South-West Pacific was a 'colonial appropriation': a sort of dolls-house arrangement where the French could just pick and choose which of the various exotic natives they ruled over were going to be put on stage, even in this day and age.

This is not to take an automatically pro-independence or anti-French line. Many small island states are quite unviable by themselves, and often seek some kind of quasi-colonial protector even when nominally independent: that's just a fact of life. But the dangers of ending up in a patronising relationship are something to bear in mind.

We toured around the islands and kayaked the beaches. Everywhere we went there were seagulls screeching and crying as they flew about. I managed to find a quiet spot to have a beach-nap and, just as I was drifting off to sleep, I saw something slithering towards me. A local came running over to me and told me to move quickly, it was a snake. Not just any snake though; a very poisonous green snake. I scarpered.

In the 1960s former French President Georges Pompidou visited New Caledonia on his way to visit the nuclear testing facilities in Tahiti. Though he spent a lot of time mending fractured relations between the various colonies of France and the metropolitan power, there's still a lot of political instability today between the pro-independents and French Loyalists. I went to the Pompidou Museum to learn a little more. I was absolutely appalled.

1930s postcards showed beautifully-dressed Tahitian, Hawaiian and Māori women. But the local Melanesian women were all depicted as 'savages' photographed in unflattering poses surrounded by children. It was clear to see that back then the Melanesians were viewed as uncivilised, whereas other islanders from the eastern Pacific, who were lighter-skinned, and also less distinct from Europeans in terms of their facial features, somewhat Asian in appearance (being related to Malays or Indonesians), were seen in a skewed romanticised view.

This is a familiar prejudice. Melanesian literally means 'from the islands of the blacks'. For a long time it was held that those who had the misfortune not to be white were at least better off being light brown and more or less Asian-looking like a Tahitian or a New Zealand Māori or a Malay, rather than a black person with frizzy hair — the typical Melanesian appearance.

Nouméa was full of fancy (boring) hotels and resorts like Club Med. I couldn't wait to leave. Maree and I headed to another island, Lifou, which is the largest and most populous island in the Îles Loyauté.

We ended up staying in a traditional Melanesian hut, made entirely from materials found in the surrounding forest. Here we got to experience real local life, not some overpriced and overcrowded hotel that seemed cut off from the local people. The local family we stayed with was very welcoming. I actually learned a lot about the local history and even about the native Māori of New Zealand.

I found out that the New Zealand Māori were originally part of the Lapita people, who had travelled from China through Melanesia and eventually made their way down to New Zealand.

The distinction between eastern Pacific peoples including the Māori, who are collectively known as Polynesians ('people from the many islands'), and the more westerly Melanesians ('people from the islands of the blacks'), is not completely fixed. There was certainly plenty of intermarriage along the way, and these seafaring peoples were forever visiting distant archipelagos in a deliberate fashion. The notion that the distinction between Melanesia and Polynesia can be upheld in any completely hard and fast manner reflects an old-fashioned obsession with ethnic racial classifications, of a sort that would nowadays be judged as rather unwholesome, and which also crumbles somewhat in the face of a reality of back-and-forth migrations, some ancient and some more modern.

Indeed, some of the local families where I stayed were actually of Māori descent, the product of a more recent reverse migration which I was extremely surprised by. They told me about how they had visited New Zealand quite a number of times: how they'd been to Rotorua and gotten to know many Māori people in the tourism industry in New Zealand.

The lady we were staying with was off to visit some friends, so she left her son to cook for us. I remember the delicious island meals he made for us from coconut crabs, with the biggest pincers I'd ever seen. They were strong enough to open a coconut shell to get to the sweet white flesh inside the fruit. He also cooked us pig and told us that all the pigs on their island are fed coconut, so we were eating coconut pig! It was so juicy and succulent.

The son told me that walking around after six o'clock at night wasn't safe for women. Apparently there were many stories of village women being raped by drunken men. He said the only way to stay safe is to make sure you have young children with you. So, I rounded up some of the local kids and we all went for a walk.

While we were wandering around I met a man who lived in the South of France, but I had a sneaking suspicion he was up to no good. I was right. He was planting marijuana with some of the locals! He invited me to go along (which I did purely out of curiosity). I ended up helping carry the bamboo pole-stakes to the area. I was a bit nervous, but because it wasn't something I'd ever done before it was a little exciting.

Even though it was time to leave New Caledonia, I wasn't done with island-hopping. My next stop was the picturesque Polynesian country of the Cook Islands.

CHAPTER EIGHTEEN
Rarotonga

A friend of mine from childhood, Dianna Ataera, was from the island of Rarotonga in the Cook Islands: so I'd always wanted to go there. Where I grew up in Hawke's Bay there was a large Rarotongan community, many of them settled in farming communities in the 1950s in places like Waipawa. Dianna's father was half Samoan and half Rarotongan, and he lived on the island most of the time. I was always captivated by his stories. I finally found time to visit.

Most tourists, and many locals, use scooters to get around because the island isn't big. It's only eleven kilometres long with one ring road that goes around the whole island. You could almost walk around the whole island in a day.

I ended up at a local stone marae, which is different to the wooden New Zealand Māori marae: but they're both sacred places with historical significance. The one I came across had eerie sacrificial stones everywhere and was over two thousand years old. There was also a canoe there that had apparently sailed to New Zealand and back.

The Cook Island language is officially known as Cook Island Māori and is extraordinarily similar to New Zealand Māori. When the Māori King from New Zealand visits Rarotonga he has no trouble communicating because the language is so similar.

I hired a motorbike and thought that because it's a small safe slow island,

I didn't need to bother with hiring a helmet. Anyway, so I'm zooming around with no helmet thinking how clever I was and the next thing I know, I'm lying on the road with the motorbike on its side. My bike hit a pothole (the roads aren't in great condition) and I fell off and smashed my head into the road. It hurt. A lot. I learned that even if you think you don't need a helmet, wear one just in case!

One of the best things about Rarotonga for someone with a New Zealand bank account is that you can use your New Zealand EFTPOS card at any of the shops. And even though there is a Rarotongan currency, you can use New Zealand money as well.

Rarotonga is an island of contrasts. Alongside all the fancy resorts and boutique hotels there's a lot of poverty. It's a Christian nation and all the locals go to church on a Sunday, but then a lot of them go and drink alcohol straight afterwards. I was surprised to discover there's a major problem with methamphetamine drugs on the island.

Foreigners aren't allowed to buy land in the Cook Islands. If you purchase a property you lease the land it is on from a local family, a lease which gets passed through the generations. I thought it was a brilliant idea because it means that land stays within the family. A new law was brought in recently saying that you can't claim your part of the land without getting every single living family member's signatures.

The Cook Islands group is made up of many small islands and atolls. I visited the picture-perfect, much-romanticised island of Aitutaki. At only eighteen square kilometres, it's even smaller than Rarotonga. I was able to walk around the whole island at a leisurely pace over grass and bush and saw pigs, fruit and flowers everywhere. The native flower, the tiare is similar to a frangipani. The long stretches of glistening white sand all along the coast made it easy to see why so many people want to get married there.

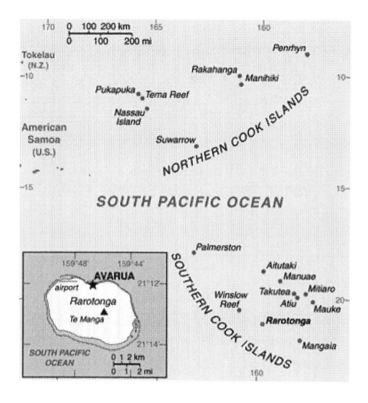

I stayed with an older retired couple who were originally from Manukau in Auckland. They were there to teach the locals how to grow food and showed me how to plant and harvest pineapple and taro. A lot of people say Aitutaki is expensive, but it wasn't. I had a room of my own with an en-suite bathroom, which only cost $15 a night. The only downside was another tourist who drove me nuts!

I spent a week there and was fascinated to hear anecdotal stories from the locals. One told me that all the local men were ditching their Cook Island wives for Australian ones. I could tell this made her a little sad... I met a great German girl there and we headed back to Rarotonga together to stay in a backpacker's hostel in Muri.

I found some of the beaches around Rarotonga were quite rough and dangerous, so I didn't go swimming there. But I did spend time on a few locals' boats, and even a day-cruise tour.

I got on so well with the locals I was even offered a job as the principal of a local school! But, I couldn't imagine living there all year-round. I'm not really a beach person so the idea of living on such a small island completely surrounded by water didn't interest me at all; I'm more of a mountain girl. The heat was another thing too; it gets really hot there: it's rare that the temperature drops below 20 degrees Celsius. I don't mind the heat but not for too long.

I met some guys from Taranaki in New Zealand, and two girls from France. We explored and hung out together. A recent storm had completely destroyed the paua and pearl oyster farms, which was sad. Black pearls are used in lots of jewellery on the island. Almost every store has black pearl bracelets, necklaces or rings.

We climbed the only sizeable peak on the island, Maunga Pu, which simply means 'top of the mountain' and is also affectionately called the Needle. We were nearly at the top when one of the guys yelled "Watch out for the monkeys!" Everyone freaked out and started running away, but then stopped when they heard him laughing. He was only joking. Half of our group got really upset with him but I thought it was hilarious.

Land mammals are rare in the South Pacific. The islands are all a pretty long swim from anywhere, and, for that reason, were generally inhabited by birds before people arrived, along with whatever reptiles and insects could survive bobbing around on a log for months. This was even true of New Zealand to a large extent. So, there certainly aren't any monkeys in the Cook Islands!

CHAPTER NINETEEN

Return to Europe

I was off to Greece and Turkey to catch up with an old friend and colleague of mine, Doug Taylor. We'd planned to spend four months in Europe together, then head down to Egypt and Jerusalem before returning to New Zealand. But then I fell in love with a saxophone player called Andy, so my plans changed a bit.

Doug and I still went to Athens, but I didn't enjoy the vibe there. I'd expected to see soft whitewashed adobe-style buildings with a cerulean blue ocean backdrop. Not in Athens; it's tacky, very hot and rocky. I found the attitude towards tourism hostile; beds in hostels and hotels would go to the highest bidder. After three nights in a reasonably-priced hotel, the manager told us the room had gone up. Instead of paying the increased price, which was considerably more than what we'd negotiated, we checked out. It was a disappointing first introduction to Greece.

One night at a restaurant run by Serbians, a man approached Doug and said that unless we paid him €200 he would hurt me. I was terrified. And horrified. Doug, of course, being a gentleman, paid the "fine" and we got out of there as quickly as we could. I guess running a "restaurant" without having to cook any food makes for good (but warped) business sense. It was extremely unsettling.

Greece felt like a major rip-off and the plumbing was a nightmare. You aren't allowed to flush toilet paper down the toilet: instead you place your used tissue into a bucket next to the loo. It was disgusting. Utterly disgusting.

On top of the unease and disappointment I felt there it was also tinged with sadness. I'd grown up thinking that this was an amazing place with a fascinating civilisation, but the Greek museums didn't appear to have many original ancient artefacts. The originals are kept in the Tate and British museums. I'd seen more Greek statues in the Vatican City than in the country where they came from.

But of course only Greece has the ancient citadel of the Acropolis and its crowning glory, the Parthenon. Yes they're ruins, but the fact that there is still anything to see at all after more than 2,400 years is incredible.

We did manage to find that classic Greek experience though on the island of Patmos. It was relaxed: not as young and boozy as Athens, with fewer tourists and more culture. Patmos is mentioned in the Bible's Book of Revelation.

St. John the Apostle, one of the twelve apostles, is traditionally supposed to have penned the Book of Revelations on Patmos: though modern scholars have concluded that the author was in truth a later figure banished to the island during persecutions of Christians at the height of the Roman Empire, two hundred years after Jesus. Either way Patmos has become a destination for pilgrims, including many Greek Australians.

There are several churches dedicated to St. John of Patmos, whoever he was, and you can visit the cave in which he is said to have written the Book of Revelations, a book that has always been a favourite of mine even if it is also hard to make much sense of.

In 1803 the German romantic Friedrich Hölderlin honoured St. John in a poem called Patmos, which famously begins "*Nah ist / Und schwer zu fassen der Gott*," or 'The God is near, and hard to grasp'.

After Patmos we headed to Rhodes, a small spearhead-shaped island, which like many of the Greek Islands is closer to Turkey than to mainland Greece. Rhodes is the home of one of the seven wonders of the ancient world. The thirty-metre Colossus of Rhodes statue straddled the harbour greeting sailors for fifty-four years, until it was destroyed by an earthquake in 226 BC.

Rhodes has one of the largest medieval towns in Europe. The town is an impressive collection of beautifully restored gothic buildings, roads, fortresses, and a castle, the Palace of the Grand Master.

The villages on Rhodes were sublime: rows of brilliant white mud houses with rounded edges overlooking the Aegean Sea. It was stunning. But it was here that I heard one of the most disturbing stories of all my adventures. A man we met told us that he'd been drugging tourists, mostly Russian women, and taking them home. He was working as a barman so he had unfettered access to their drinks. He then asked if I wanted a beer! As soon as Doug returned from the bathroom we left. I never told him about the Greek Freak.

I hadn't enjoyed Greece. For that reason, I couldn't wait to get to Turkey.

TURKEY

We took the train from Athens to Turkey to save money. It would have taken just over an hour to fly there, but by rail it took us twelve hours. We drank a lot of beer. So, I can't remember anything about the landscape.

We eventually arrived in Istanbul and I remember wondering where all the women in head scarves and burqas were? Because Turkey is a Muslim country, I assumed that women would be modestly dressed. But Istanbul is a very modern western-style city, a city of surprises. These days there probably are more head scarves; but that was then.

I was interested to see the Turkish people had more Mongolian features than Arabic. For of course the Turks are of central Asian origin, and completely unrelated to most other Middle Eastern peoples. I hadn't known that to begin with.

I was also surprised to learn — clearly I didn't know much about the actual diversity of the Middle East! — that the most conspicuous of Istanbul's mosques had begun its existence as a Christian cathedral, originally erected in the later years of the Roman Empire. Ayasofia is the Turkish version of the building's original Greek name of Hagia Sophia, meaning 'blessed wisdom'. After the city was captured by the Turkish-dominated Ottoman Empire in 1453, the cathedral of Hagia Sophia became the mosque of Ayasofia.

Many of its mosaics and specifically Christian features were covered with plaster, though the building was otherwise preserved and even strengthened against earthquakes under Ottoman rule. Since the 1930s Ayasofia has been a secular museum, and when I was there a full-scale renovation and restoration was under way. Shimmering, colourful marble mosaics lined the inside of the great dome, nearly fifty-six metres high on the *inside*. It is a sight to behold.

We travelled down the Aegean coast stopping at little hostels along the way. One hostel owner suggested I marry him and become his second wife. I didn't think that being a sister-wife was an attractive proposition so politely declined. I was surprised how much he looked like one of the New Zealand Māori people; the thing about travel is that you notice the differences and similarities to what you know, everywhere you go.

At another small coastal village I saw a family of traditional Muslim women dressed in hijabs. The four year old daughter reached up and pulled the grandmother's hijab off her head! The mother didn't know what to do because she was holding a baby and the grandmother was frantically trying to recover her hair. She was very annoyed and told the little girl off. I couldn't stop laughing, despite the fact that they were glaring at me. No-one else was laughing: no doubt by their standards I was very impolite.

Aside from that one moment of embarrassment, I was welcomed, greeted and treated warmly everywhere I went in Turkey. The Turkish people love New Zealanders and a surprising number of people I met had family in New Zealand. I wonder whether it's because we have such a strong connection to the Turkish through the war and the tragic events at Gallipoli.

The rug industry is huge in Turkey: if you ever need a carpet get one here. Even though they're on sale on every corner, the sales people weren't as pushy as they were in other parts of the world I've visited.

I'm a huge fan of Mustafa Kemal Ataturk, the first President of Turkey. He led his country out of the ashes of the Ottoman Empire to create the Republic of Turkey. His last name actually means 'Father of Turks' and, since he was gifted the name in 1934, no one else is allowed to be called that. He was a revolutionist, and after World War I he built thousands of schools, made education free and gave women equal rights.

I fell in love with Turkey and the people: it was such a contrast of old and modern, and an absolute mine of historic places and sites. I had desperately wanted to visit the ancient Christian Caves to the south of Istanbul which dated back to the 6th Century BC, but we just ran out of time. One day I'll go back and stay for longer.

But travelling is expensive and I needed to earn some money. So, I headed to London to get back into teaching.

CHAPTER TWENTY
Teaching in London

I found a job teaching at a high school in Brentwood in Essex, north of London. I only had five students in my class, all of whom were clinically disturbed, and for the most part I did enjoy it. But it was tough. And before long I was dealing with issues not too different from those I faced when teaching in New Zealand.

One boy threatened to hit me. I went to the principal and demanded that he be removed from my class: no one deserves to put up with that behaviour in the classroom. Yet instead of the situation being resolved, the same boy bashed the principal. He was suspended for a week, but then a week later was back at school. In my class! I didn't sign up to be a cop without a weapon (at least the police have truncheons) and after a series of stalking incidents involving another student I left.

Soho is one of my favourite places in London: full of food, jazz, music and interesting people. I had Jewish food for the first time there and loved it! But the problem with London is that from November it gets darker and darker. The sun sets at 3:30 in the afternoon. I just hated it — it was depressing. The tube wasn't safe after midnight so the nights were dark, long and boring. At least in the countryside you can go on full moon walks, look at the stars, ramble up mountains. But in an urban environment it's hard to survive being locked indoors every night for months.

It was nearing November, and after four months I was ready to go home.

Andy the saxophone player came with me for a little while. But he preferred the hustle and bustle of London to the quiet life in New Zealand.

CHAPTER TWENTY-ONE
Ohhhhh Canada

I N 2003 I went with my friend Sam to Vancouver, Canada. He was originally from there and was taking me to meet his family. Sam lived with some friends in the small city of Chilliwack, just east of Vancouver.

The night we arrived there was a Foo Fighters concert at an inner-city venue called the Plaza of Nations. Before we headed off, Sam and his friends cooked a traditional dinner of tinfoil-wrapped halibut with courgettes, carrots, garlic and tomatoes on the BBQ. I'd never had halibut before; it was delicious.

It was my first night out in Vancouver and it ended up being quite the introduction. We were walking back to the carpark after seeing an amazing concert (the energy level of the Foo Fighters on stage was infectious) when a guy approached us frothing at the mouth and holding a knife. We quickly moved in the opposite direction. Sam told me he was a drug addict trying to rob cars and get money for his habit. I was astounded.

But drugs weren't the only problem. The city was being destroyed by high-density housing. In my opinion it made Vancouver look a bit like a slum. Or maybe that was just because the bit we had travelled through from Sam's place to the Plaza of Nations was mostly East Vancouver, notorious for being the rougher and less touristy part of town.

I didn't realise how close we were to the USA. We drove along the border where you could see the boats coming into Canada from the United States of America.

It was busy. And amazing. They had gondolas and railway cars that would take you up the mountain to the Whistler ski resort so you didn't even need a car. Once you got to the top there were stacks of ski lodges, resorts and restaurants ranging from budget to fine-dining.

As amazing as Whistler was, there were a number of buildings being demolished. When I asked why Sam told me that they were all leaky buildings, just like they were building in New Zealand. I could have ripped my hair out! Vancouver had had this problem already, and now we were doing the same in Auckland (but that's another story).

We hopped into a canoe to paddle down the river and I saw ravens for the first time. Such glossy back feathers make them beautiful birds. And smart too — they can cleverly steal food in ways you couldn't imagine.

Sam wanted to take us to his father's place in a town called Hope, further inland from Chilliwack. Hope reminded me so much of New Zealand, particularly the Coromandel and the South Island: it's filled with waterfalls and dense bush areas. I'd known Sam for several years since meeting him in Sumner near Christchurch and I could now understand why he loved New Zealand's South Island so much. It reminded him of home.

I lost hope in Hope. It was supposed to be summer there and there was a five-week gale! But his father's place was gorgeous. He had twenty dairy cows on his property and hundreds of beautiful red hummingbirds flittering around. They're my favourite birds. Brian's Dad used to put bowls of honey out for them and they would come inside and dart around the house.

We headed to stay at Sam's mother's house on the optimistically named Sunshine Coast of British Columbia, north of Vancouver. The Sunshine Coast includes places with names like Desolation Inlet, which is the sort of name you come across in the remote sub-Antarctic southwest region of New Zealand known as Fiordland in English or the Atawhenua, the 'Shadowland', in Māori. However the Sunshine Coast actually does get plenty of sunshine, as the long and mountainous Vancouver Island to the west intercepts most of the bad weather.

I thought the Sunshine Coast of British Columbia was a beautiful place — just like the Atawhenua, but with more sunshine — and I could see why Sam's mother wanted to live there surrounded by native bush and armies of driftwood along the beach. Sam's brother was living there too, in a shed out the back.

Sam's mother was really lovely and I remember her making a Canadian beef delicacy for us. It was fattening but tasty. She'd smother beef in tomato sauce, soy and garlic and bake it on a low temperature. I still eat this dish now on occasion.

Sam's brother was not only using marijuana but growing it too. And he had a semi-automatic AK-47 assault rifle for "protection," which made me a lot more nervous than if he hadn't.

We were out walking one day and I casually mentioned that I'd love to see a black bear. Well the next thing I know Sam's brother runs away,

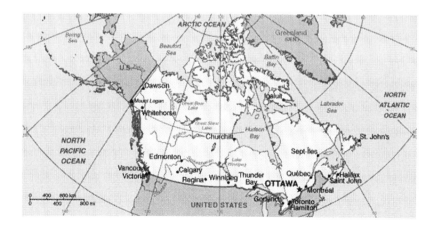

returns with his gun and says he's going to shoot one! I was not impressed. I was astounded that it was just so normal to go out and shoot them. No one seemed bothered by it. You could get hunting permits there to go and shoot grizzly bears! I couldn't understand why. At least in some respects there was controlled hunting for grizzly bears. But you could shoot black bears whenever you saw one, just like how they shoot possums in New Zealand.

I got to see the home that Sam and his family had grown up in. I was amazed because the house was sitting directly under low hanging powerlines: that wasn't good.

While we were there it was Sam's fortieth birthday and he had a big party with some friends and all his family. I got to meet his adopted sister and a close cousin who told me a lot about the challenges she faced being a social worker working with drug addicts. She said it was an almost-daily practice to give addicts an injection that would disrupt their overdose and bring them out of their drugged stupor. She told me to be careful in Vancouver East where the drug problems had gotten quite bad recently. I told her I'd already had an introduction to it!

We ferried to Mayne Island and I learned first-hand what tree sitters were. A group of environmental activists were sitting in the trees protesting deforestation. I could understand why — the wildlife here was amazing. We saw a 500 year-old eagle's nest and black bears along the shoreline picking up rocks along the beach looking for shellfish.

There was a nude beach on the island, but even thought I'd spent two years naked on the Chinese junk I wasn't keen to be perved on by creepy old men with saggy balls selling hash cakes. I kept my clothes on. And I stayed away from the crazies.

We headed back to Vancouver and Brian went to visit friends so I checked into a hostel. For some reason the hostel owners would change the locks on you all the time: it was very annoying. Even though I had been warned to avoid Vancouver East, that's where the cheapest hostel was, so I stayed there but didn't go out at night. The last thing I wanted was another meeting with a knife-wielding drug addict.

But because I didn't feel safe, I didn't stay there long. I headed off on the train through the Rockies to Banff. It was a long trip, nearly a thousand kilometres, but it was beautiful. The train weaved through mountainous ranges, tightly-packed forests and across crystal clear rivers. I couldn't have dreamed the scenery would be so incredible. The Rockies are utterly amazing.

I found a place to stay half an hour north of Banff, in a small town called Lake Louise, which is known for its turquoise lake surrounded by snowy peaks. The Fairmont Chateau at Lake Louise was a luxury hotel famous for its uninterrupted view over the lake and the Victoria Glacier. It was gorgeous. I made friends with some Chinese tourists and we explored the local area together. I was blown away by the beauty of the Canadian wilderness.

As much as I loved it there it was time to start heading to Vancouver to meet up with Sam and make our way back to New Zealand.

Sadly, as dear as Sam was to me I got to understand what living with an addict would be like. He had full-blown marijuana psychosis and would have his first joint at 8am in the morning — a wake and bake. He'd top himself up during the day and by the end of our trip together I could see that it was damaging to who he was as a person. He'd become a shell: a very confused and deluded individual. I decided that I wouldn't travel with him again.

CHAPTER TWENTY-TWO

New Zealand for Another Minute

I N 2002, I created my own business training teachers. There was a huge shortage in Auckland and the language market in New Zealand had ballooned out with record numbers of non-English speaking immigrants. The quality of teachers available to teach English as a second language ('ESL') was appalling. But I didn't just deal with ESL schools: there were also many private hospitality, computing and nursing schools too. Most of these schools were not regulated by the Government and many schools went under owing lots of money to disappointed teachers and students.

Since 1987 the fourth Labour Government, under the guise of Rogernomics — a free market economic plan — had discussed increasing the population of New Zealand to around five million as well as selling New Zealand land and citizenship to the world. Actually, this seemed like a plan to create a Malthusian sort of society that would benefit the landowner most of all. I remember being warned by my lecturers of the likelihood of a return to the Victorian era of low wages and homelessness.

Starting a business at that time was tough. I'd paid Telecom (now Spark) $2100 for advertising and an assurance that the internet would work from where I lived in Auckland. It turned out that the internet didn't work and all the money I spent on advertising went down the gurgler because I couldn't access the web. Contractors they sent out to the house were useless and pervy (they insinuated that "special favours" could get the internet up and running instantly). It was creepy. And disruptive to the business I'd just started. It took twelve years for Telecom to fix the local exchange and get business-quality internet in the area.

I finally launched the business and it was hard yakka. I was working seventy-hour weeks on average. It then became increasingly competitive because I believed in paying teachers $20 an hour, and charging them out at $28. Some of the other larger companies would pay their teachers $15, but charge them out at $28 an hour or more. There was more money in the margins but I wasn't prepared to pay my teachers less, let alone deal with language schools that didn't respect teaching staff.

I diversified and started providing specialty teachers. I was poaching leading chefs from the hospitality sector and getting them into teaching roles. I started doing permanent placements and poached people from cold-calling in different industries. I tended to make quite a bit more money that way.

At one time, I had sixty or seventy people on my books. There was such a scarcity of teachers that I actually started training people. For people to get permanent residency they had to score a six in the English literacy test. But I believe it had a lot to do with the luck on the day; if you had an interest in science and the test that day was mostly science-related then you'd probably be a New Zealand citizen. If the exam was about politics and your political knowledge was on point you'd generally get through it as well. The reverse was also true. Business migrants were welcomed into New Zealand if they had a million New Zealand dollars or its equivalent in their bank account. But this of course resulted in a number of scams being uncovered in which immigration consultants would just transfer money from one account to the next, collecting a fee for their efforts.

My business was thriving. I was able to put away some money and buy another rental property in the up-and-coming but not-quite-there-yet suburb of Point Chevalier in Auckland.

The language school industry in New Zealand was in a fair bit of strife. Many courses were being created by untrustworthy and unprofessional people. Students were arriving (mostly from China) to attend language schools and stay with host families and there'd be no food (or substandard food) and no teachers. There were many language schools in the heart of Auckland that didn't even have a kitchen or a social area for the students to cook or sit down together.

In spite of the huge shortage of qualified teaching staff, I found a few fantastic former teachers from secondary schools. I brought together a good crop of really qualified people who could draw up courses in subjects such as travel and tourism and accountancy, as well as ESL.

CHAPTER TWENTY-THREE
It's a-ok in the UK

I was after a place that cost under $45 a night. I used a website called Rates to Go that was the Airbnb of 2008. It just goes to show how booking and travels change: you need to keep ahead of those changes to get good deals. The accommodation was okay until I started hearing rats at night, chewing through the floorboards.

It was snowing when I was in London. In April. Not usually a month that brings snow. I hired a rental car for $21 a day because I acquired the deal outside of New Zealand. I was thrilled with the price for a fortnight but shocked when the congestion tax was charged. I got three fines and had to pay $260 in congestion tax!

One of the most surprising discoveries in London was Churchill's War Rooms, an underground bunker around the corner from the Prime Minister's residence at 10 Downing Street. Churchill lived in the bunker while he was directing the United Kingdom's World War II efforts, complete with a Map Room and a Cabinet Room that was used 24/7. Apparently more than a hundred top-secret meetings were held here. I was blown away by this place; it still had the mattress he slept on and all the equipment they used in that era plus a map showing where his armed forces were stationed. But it didn't appear to be on the tourist radar. Many of my friends had never even heard of it!

Being in London close to the West End was fantastic. I saw comedy shows, musicals and the wonderful Miss Saigon. And being just a short walk from snow-covered Hyde Park was amazing! Even though I'd been to London several times this was my favourite visit. It just goes to show that there's always something new to be discovered, even when you think you've done (and seen) it all.

But I had itchy feet (again) so I embarked on a road trip.

The plan was to head to Dundee, eight hours drive north, but I got lost on the A1 and ended up in Sherwood Forest, six hours south of where I meant to be.

Naturally, I had to look for Robin Hood. The thing about Sherwood Forest is that there's an entire tourism industry built on the legend of Mr. Hood so it didn't take long to find the Major Oak, the tree that allegedly hid the robber from his arch-nemesis, the Sheriff of Nottingham.

There's some debate whether the "steal from the rich and give to the poor" stories dating back to the 1400s are real. Regardless, it's a great story. Recently it's been suggested that Robin Hood was a character that outlaws adopted: kind of like wearing a mask or a costume to conceal their true identity. Who did it? Why, Robin Hood did it!

After a night in a log cabin in the forest I got up early and tried to get to Dundee. I say tried, because I got lost. Again. And ended up in Kendal, four hours south of where I'd planned to be!

I headed north once more, figuring eventually driving in that direction would take me to where I wanted. But instead I ended up in the Lake District. Not quite all the way north, but somewhere up that way.

The Lake District was like being in an Edwardian Beatrix Potter book, and funnily enough it was home to the famous children's author.

Ms. Potter stayed at Wray Castle in the region when she was sixteen for a summer, which sparked a lifelong love affair with the countryside. And

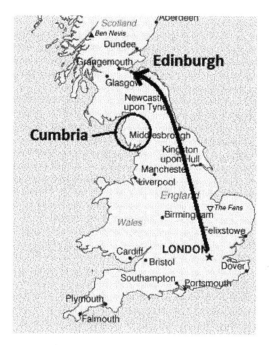

My approximately intended route from London to Edinburgh,
and where I ended up after getting lost...
(Map drawn for this book using thumbnail from World Factbook*)*

in later years she wrote many of her books from her farm here and they haven't stopped selling. Around two million books are sold each year; that's four books every minute. And I could see why she chose to write here: it's a peaceful and inspiring place. When Beatrix died she left fifteen farms and four thousand acres to the National Trust; so this area really is Potter-land, full of rolling hills, idyllic cottages and, of course, more lakes than you can shake a stick at. I had no idea that the United Kingdom had so many beautiful national parks. I'd always considered the country to be an urban society, so was delighted to see that the monarch (and the Government) had gifted large tracts of land to be enjoyed by the public. I finally made it to Dundee, a week later, and was excited to stay with my aunt and uncle. I knew it was their house when I saw a sign saying "Haere Mai" on the garden gate. They're always so welcoming and hospitable, but their enthusiasm led to an evening of herbicide.

We were at the local bowling club when my uncle started plying me, and everyone around us, with whisky. Every time his back was turned I sneakily tipped it into the plant. We were there for hours. Everyone was drunk on whisky, including the plants. The next morning I was so glad to not have a hangover I drove to Wales to continue my journey.

WALES

My first stop was Llangadog, situated in the Towy Valley. Wales is full of sheep and sheepdogs, and the local pub was full of sheep farmers. It reminded me of rural New Zealand.

An hour south is Swansea, where I headed next. It is the second largest city in Wales after Cardiff. I loved Swansea. There was free internet in all the buses and libraries, which in 2008 was quite unusual.

Oystermouth Castle was a particular highlight. Built early in the twelfth century by the Normans it was captured, fought over, damaged and rebuilt many times over the centuries that followed. It was in ruined and decayed condition but still fascinating as being a centre of local heritage. I understand it's since had an extensive refurbishment so it would be nice to revisit one day and see how different it looks.

I headed down the coast to Cornwall, stopping in Torquay on the English Riviera. It's famous throughout England for two reasons: it was the home of bestselling novelist Agatha Christie and the inspiration for John Cleese's

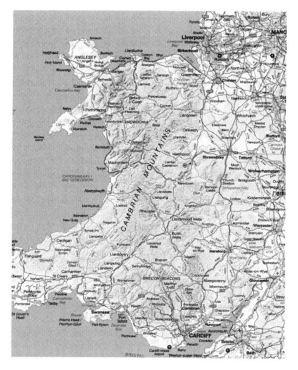

*Wales (*Mapmoose*)*

most famous character, Basil Fawlty, based on a Torquay hotelier.

I was surprised by how cheap property prices were in Torquay. For $240,000 you could get a beautiful house with an established garden.

I even saw one property with New Zealand ponga, or giant tree ferns, survivors of the Carboniferous era of fossil antiquity. By English standards the ponga looks like something that belongs in a hot-house and probably does in Britain, anywhere outside of Torquay at any rate.

Much more common throughout Britain is the New Zealand cabbage tree, a general term for species of the genus *Cordyline*. These look like North American yuccas, though they are not related to yuccas. The cabbage tree's name comes from an early confusion with certain tropical palms whose

Cousin Charlie with a parrot, perching on his dog

leaves were often eaten as a vegetable by sailors in Captain Cook's day. Cook's crew thought the New Zealand cabbage trees were the same, but they weren't!

The established leaves of New Zealand cabbage trees take a long time to rot and have horse-tails of long, tough fibre staples inside them. This creates problems for those trying to keep their gardens looking tidy or to mow lawns beneath a cabbage tree. In fact scientists are interested in using these long, tough, stringy fibres as a natural fibre in resin composites!

It is true that some of the inner leaves can be cooked and eaten along with other parts of the tree. But by and large the *New Zealand* cabbage tree is not good eating compared to its namesakes.

Most New Zealand plants and birds are known by their Māori names these days. Though pioneers often gave them English names, these generally didn't last.

Thus the creature the first British settlers named the parson-bird, with its black plumage and little white neck-ruff, eventually came to be known to all by its Māori name of the Tūī; the white pine became the Kahikatea once again; and so on.

But the utterly misleading name of cabbage tree stuck with cordylines, known to Māori as Tī, perhaps because Tī sounded like something else to the settlers, something you definitely couldn't make from a cabbage tree.

Cabbage trees are known in Britain as Torquay Palms. This made me jealous because I had tried to grow one of a particular type that caught my eye in Torquay in my own back garden in New Zealand, and failed. Even the tough-as-old-boots cordyline can be a bit fussy about where it is grown.

After all the travelling and driving, I needed a quick family fix. So, I headed to Bath to see my cousin Charlie and his hunter beagle Sniffer.

Charlie was saving money and was operating a mini-sanctuary for neglected macaw parrots out of his house. Apparently during the 1970s it was fashionable to have a pet parrot in your lounge. Owners would clip (or break) their wings so they couldn't fly away, but after a few years when the fad died out hundreds of parrots were abandoned. They live for around fifty years in captivity so they're a lifelong responsibility. A local aviary had been looking after them but they'd run out of funding and space, so bird-lover Charlie had taken them in. He had around a hundred birds, a handful of which were elderly macaws.

IRELAND

After so much driving I decided to fly to Ireland to catch up with my friend James of the fluctuating weight, who'd in the meantime built a successful gluten-free sauce and cracker company in Limerick.

Ireland has a buzz about it. The last time I'd been there the infrastructure was developing and Irish people were returning to Ireland. There were so many good things happening there in design, engineering, film, telecommunications and transport, despite Ireland being one of the most affected countries in the global financial crisis.

Even so, the government had neglected the absolute basics in public finance, wage policy and bank regulation since before the new millennium. So, many people were still hard done by.

My friend James' sauces were becoming very popular, but it was hard work. James was driving the trucks about sixty hours a week just to meet orders, on top of everything else required to run a business. He'd put on weight once more due to a combination of stress and the sauces, no doubt, and was exhausted.

Ina and John, my friends from Bali, came to see me and we all went to see James' trade show at a 5-star hotel. Afterwards we all went for dinner and there were some disheartening topics discussed.

John said that he wasn't making any money with his dairying, mainly because his herd was so small, about a tenth of the size of New Zealand herds. And that amount would most likely be reduced once the European Union got rid of the subsidies. Nobody was drinking, which made quite a change from the last time I'd caught up with my friends!

While I was there I made the decision to close down my business. I was owed a lot of money and after calling in all the debts I shut operations down. That was just in the nick of time. The recession happened and I managed to avoid losses. Luckily my properties retained their value.

CHAPTER TWENTY-FOUR
All Roads Lead Around Rome

I flew to La Rochelle, a small port-city on the southwest coast of France, famous throughout Europe for its sustainability and student-culture.

I was staying with my ex Niels from *Elf-Chine*. He'd been through a bad patch: he'd lost his job, his fiancée, and nearly everything in his apartment due to a fire as well. I felt very sorry for him.

We spent a lovely few days together then headed to Paris to visit the old *Elf-Chine*, moored on the River Seine since 1995 and now reverted to the name of *La Dame de Canton*.

The junk owners had sold it to a buyer that turned it into a floating restaurant for a few years. And though we all thought the boat would one day go back to the ocean, the cost of getting it seaworthy was exorbitant. But it was river-worthy, hence its location on the Seine. Now it's a nightclub and party venue, available to PR companies and advertising agencies to hire. Being back on it bought back a flood of emotions and memories — I found it a bit sad that the junk was no longer sailing around the world.

Niels' son and I danced all night on the junk at a house-music party. Niels didn't understand or enjoy the music (which made me laugh).

France at the time was suffering through the recession. There were huge levels of unemployment, homelessness and crime: I had my iPhone stolen.

I love Paris and there are a few places that I wanted to see while I was there. I had secured a hotel, which wasn't very nice at $40 a night. I spent the first day just walking through all the manicured gardens, so beautiful.

I went to the famous Moulin Rouge, at $100 a ticket. What an amazing experience: the choreography, along with the dancers' outfits, made the stage appear to be a piece of artwork. The artwork changed along with the choreography as well as the dancer's clothes multiple times throughout the show. It was incredible and something I would go and see again.

Anyway, I decided to do the museums and I went to the Grand Petit Palais. I loved the art work, especially pieces created during the Venetian period and the incomparable Leonardo Da Vinci. Paris is full of beautiful artistic sights, so it suited me just fine.

ITALY

I'd always loved Italy so I decided to do a little more travelling around one of my favourite countries. San Remo on the Mediterranean Coast was the first stop, to catch up with another old friend who was working on super-yachts. He had some pretty interesting stories of how the other half live, none of which I can reveal due to confidentiality, but you can imagine how ludicrous some of the demands were.

A three-hour train ride north took me to Milano (Milan) where I spent some time with an Italian couple, Lorenza and Italo. We had met in Gan in 1982, so it had been years since I'd seen them.

Lorenza's parents had come to Italy from Croatia, as refugees during World War II: they literally escaped with only the clothes on their backs.

Italo had blond hair and bright blue eyes back then but sadly he now had emphysema. However, we were so happy to see each other. He'd tried living in Cuba on a boat but got very disillusioned with Castro, even though he believed in the revolution. He'd become politically disenchanted.

I was shocked to discover that in Italy, nuclear waste was being dumped off the coast and buried in the bush! Apparently the Calabrian Mafia started disposing of toxic waste illegally in the 1980s, when few restrictions were in place and bribery was at an all-time high.

The New York Times reported that cancer rates were up to 47 per cent higher in the affected areas. They estimated that ten million tonnes of toxic and nuclear waste were buried in Italy and Germany and that at least thirty ships full of radioactive material had been sunk off the coast. Many news organisations reported that the plan was to send the toxic products to Somalia for burial, but after paying off local politicians the Mafia saved money on transportation and just stuck it in their own backyard.

Apparently some waste did make it to Africa, but warlords, bribes and illegal weapons trading were involved. No wonder the situation is called Italy's Chernobyl. You also can't help wondering what would have happened to the waste in Somalia: perhaps it would be fired right back at us by terrorists.

Lorenza and Italo lived thirty kilometres out of the city in an area where Lorenza could ride horses every day. Her horse-riding instructor used to work for Silvio Berlusconi and like the former Prime Minister had an eye for the ladies, even though they were both married. The instructor suggested we have an affair, but I wasn't interested.

My friends took me to Brescia, about ninety minutes east of where they lived. It's an area famed for its ancient religious buildings; a round cathedral affectionately called La Rotunda (but actually named Duomo Vecchio) is the highlight. Built in the sixth or seventh century over floor mosaics that some say were part of Roman baths in the first century, it's a stunningly preserved piece of architecture: one of the few examples of a circular basilica still standing. Thousands of worshippers come to pay their respects each year and to celebrate the Catholic Sacred Mysteries, named after the theory that supernatural forces united with religious leaders to make sense of unexplainable events in the Bible.

I revisited Lorenza five years later in 2013, by which time the economic collapse had become prominent and many Italian industries were closing down; Chinese ones were opening up. The locals were getting really, really annoyed. Also the bribery under Berlusconi had gone beyond comprehension.

A friend of Lorenza's niece told me a sad story about Mafia interference. Apparently, her husband, a doctor, had been living in New York but was hoping to move back to Milan to raise their children. He'd applied for a surgical role but the Mafia intercepted his CV and denied his appointment. The Mafia were so brazen; rather than just let him think he was passed over for someone more qualified or suitable, they actually called him and told him not to apply again! I still don't know why he was on their radar though. Probably a historical family thing.

My gluten intolerance flared up in Italy. All the bread, pasta and sauces were sending my digestive system into panic. And I got pretty ill. I was almost vomiting and gluten-free pizzas and pastas were hard to come by.

Lorenza had tried to live in New York, as she was a successful designer. She worked for a design company and she used to get the work done in third world countries where women needed the money. She was a really ethical employer. When I visited her in 2013, she took me to meet a guy who ran a vineyard and she helped ensure that mules and donkeys were bred in humane conditions. The EU subsidised the cause because the animals were regarded as part of Italy's heritage.

CROATIA

The train ride from Milano to Trieste, the most easterly large city in Italy, just fifteen kilometres from Slovenia, was only a short trip of five hours in total. In Trieste I caught a bus to Dubrovnik in Croatia, a trip that should have been pleasant. It wasn't. Some of the other people on the bus were really rough: I thought I was going to get beaten up.

I loved Dubrovnik, it was absolute heaven. It was an old castle city on a port. I hadn't experienced that before, so the contrast between the fifteenth century stonework, fortifications and the turquoise waters of the Adriatic Sea was stunning.

The Croatian currency of the Kuna was being stabilised with the Euro around that time so prices went up about twenty percent. The locals were not happy with the increase in food prices but I thought it was still cheaper than other places I'd visited. And the food was incredible: beautifully fresh produce and amazing herbs and spices.

From Dubrovnik, I got a ferry to the Mljet National Park, a long thin island not far from the mainland. The island was stunning; it's the oldest protected marine park in the Mediterranean, covered by a dense forest with little villages and a twelfth century monastery. It was super-cheap living in the park; you could get an omelette for a dollar. Anyone could live like a king here for a week. But the drunken boat crew would drop you out of the regal head zone pretty quickly. And they were the only option to get around, unless you could afford your own chopper.

BOSNIA AND HERZEGOVINA

On the way to Serbia I found myself passing through Bosnia and Herzegovina. I met a thirtyish Indian woman on the bus who had a pink teddy bear and I asked her where she'd been travelling.

"I won big at the Las Vegas casino and I've decided to travel and write a book about my travels," she said to me. She had travelled through India on a train with more rats than passengers and it was her second time in Bosnia and Herzegovina. She loved her teddy bear and took it everywhere! I never took a train in India because of the story she told me. I don't like rats and I don't go where they are.

I was quite shocked to find myself in Bosnia and Herzegovina because I hadn't planned on going there. I started thinking about all the images of the civil war on the TV between the Bosnian Muslims, the Croats, the Serbs and the Yugoslav Army. Eventually I got to Montenegro, I didn't really like Montenegro. The beaches were cold and everything was closed down. I thought it would be early spring during April and May but it was still as cold as anything. I felt like I was being followed so I took a hotel for $110 a night.

The next morning, I couldn't wait to get to get out of Montenegro. The train ride out was scary. Half of the carriages were in complete darkness and there were single men sitting everywhere and because their boots had been worn in the snow there were puddles everywhere. I didn't want to be sitting with strange men in the dark so I sat with families in well-lit ones. There was this one young guy in a soldier's uniform; he looked about twenty-three. I turned around and said, "How can you treat people worse than dogs? Why do you shoot people?" He erupted. "How can you criticise the army? I come from an officer's school I could arrest you right now. They breed like flies and we don't like the way they treat their women. We're sick of them."

I was just trying to understand how they could hate people to the point where they were shooting them without justification or remorse. I hadn't realised that the Serbians had an officer training school in Montenegro.

SERBIA

I finally reached Belgrade in Serbia and there was a presidential election campaign going on.

One of the candidates, Boris Tadić was more influenced by Western ideals and offered to be part of the EU. The other, Tomislav Nikolić was a lot more conservative and wanted a 'greater Serbia' and was pro-Russian with his way of politics. It was an extremely tense time because of Kosovo's proclamation of independence from Serbia and the breakdown of the coalition government.

I found being here challenging; I couldn't understand the street maps and I couldn't make sense of the Slavic language and the Cyrillic lettering: I couldn't find my way anywhere.

I stayed in a youth hostel where the guy there loved the Flight of the Conchords. When he found out I was from New Zealand I received special treatment. At the time, in Serbia a lot of people wanted to be part of the EU and at that time they could only travel to seven countries. Now they're negotiating their EU accession.

I met a guy here named Yuri who was in the army training to be an officer. He really wanted to leave Serbia; he said he wasn't happy there anymore. He took me to the bakeries and the food was disgusting; being gluten intolerant was a nightmare. Bits of pastry with spinach in it had become trendy around the world; the craze hadn't escaped Serbia either. Yuri was very keen to leave Serbia and asked if I had a niece he could marry in New Zealand.

I visited one of the major forts there called the Golubac Fortress, a 14th century fortified town on the Danube River. During the Middle Ages it was the object of many battles, especially between the Ottoman Empire and the

Kingdom of Hungary. It had been passed between the Turks, Bulgarians, Hungarians, Serbs, and Austrians, until 1867, when it was turned over to the Serbian Prince, Mihailo Obrenović III.

I stayed about five nights in Belgrade and was completely impressed by it, in spite my other negative fears and feelings. Belgrade was surprisingly green with heaps of flowers. And there were so many wooden buildings and fences. Most places I'd been had medieval stonemasonry, so it was nice to see something different. I wasn't expecting to like it but that's the lovely thing about travel; you never really know where you are going to enjoy things and where you are not.

There was a drink made from sweetcorn, a version of the famous Turkish boza, which I really liked even though it looked revolting. It was a frothy brown liquid that tasted amazing; if they'd put yellow food colouring in it would have looked much more appetising. But I guess the Serbians were

150

used to the way it looked!

Croatia has a fascinating and tortured history; from its original Roman roots in 11 BCE to one of the bloodiest events in Europe since World War II, the Bosnian War. Under former Serbian and later Yugoslav President Slobodan Milošević's rule around 100,000 people (mostly Croats, Bosnians and Muslims) were killed during a three-year period of ethnic cleansing. Milošević was vilified in the Western media and eventually arrested and charged with war crimes. He died in prison in 2006, while still on trial an incredible five years after his arrest.

One might have thought that the prisoner had gone to a just reward. Yet in a surprise ruling in 2016, Milošević was exonerated by the International Criminal Tribunal for the Former Yugoslavia in the Hague, while at the same time the leader of the Bosnian Serbs, Radovan Karadžić, was sentenced to forty years in prison. It now seems that most of the atrocities and tortures perpetrated in the Bosnian conflict had been dreamed up by local militias as things spiralled out of control, though the International Court of Justice had decided in 2007, already, that such a powerful figure as Milošević should have done more to prevent what eventually happened. He had certainly helped to whip things up in the early days as well.

It was quite difficult working out all the different currencies because many of these places were not part of the European Union at that time. I used the Euro in Trieste, the Kuna in Croatia (which it still currently uses despite being an European Union member), the Dinar in Serbia, the Euro again in Montenegro and the convertible Mark in Bosnia-Herzegovina, which replaced the Dinar in 1998.

CHAPTER TWENTY-FIVE

Dictators and Dracula

THE train took five hours from Belgrade to Sofia, the capital of Bulgaria. But arriving there was not something I'd want to repeat. The train station was deserted. And dark. Usually train stations have their own subculture of shops, eateries and many people wandering about or socialising: this was different. It wasn't a 'living' station. The underground gave me a strange feeling.

I stayed in a hostel run by an old flirty guy who was a jazz musician. He offered to take me around Sofia, but as I suspected that it would come with a few 'special offers', I declined.

The hostel was weird. There were about fifteen Americans staying there at the time but there was something about them that I hadn't experienced before.

They all looked military or ex-military and were dressed the same even though they weren't in a uniform. They were wearing the kind of civilian clothes that came out of a government wardrobe. They were constantly drunk and seemed dodgy. The hostel's owner confided in me that they were all CIA so I stayed clear of them!

I didn't stay long in Bulgaria. Some people have really liked the place but they must have seen other parts than me. I thought it was time to move on. So I did.

EASTERN ROMANIA

I headed five hours north on the train past four nuclear power plants that looked so old they should have been decommissioned, to Bucharest, the capital of Romania.

I'd had a massage therapist in Auckland from Romania, who had escaped there in 1980 and had never been back: I was keen to see where she came from.

Living under the dictatorship of Nicolae Ceausescu must have been next-level. Under his communist 'leadership' he'd ordered the murders of around 60,000 people, caused food shortages by sending most of the country's food overseas and forced the country's many orphanages into complete disrepair, leaving the children living in horribly unsanitary and unsafe conditions. He was eventually arrested, tried in a one-hour trial, and executed along with his influential wife, whom some say was the real power behind the throne, for their crimes. Apparently the last words he ever uttered were, "Long live the Socialist Republic of Romania! History will avenge me!" It hasn't. Romania has struggled to recover from his quarter-century at the helm.

I got a chance to visit his former palace: an outrageously- sized imposing building. Built in 1984, it's the world's heaviest building and the third-largest building in the world: which gives you an idea of how ridiculously grandiose it was. It's currently valued at $3.3 billion making it the world's most expensive administrative building. Lighting and heating the building costs nearly $8 million a year alone — money that could have been better spent elsewhere under the dictator's regime.

I've always been fascinated with churches, in particular Orthodox churches. But I found this one in Bucharest a bit strange.

I wanted to buy a picture of the black Madonna with baby Jesus. In countries with Roman Catholic and Eastern Orthodox majorities, images of the Virgin Mary and baby Jesus with black or dark skin are common. There are all kinds of theories as to why this is so, including the idea that many Europeans in the Middle Ages thought that anyone from the Middle East had to be black! Later on Jesus would be represented as decidedly light-skinned with long golden hair, and the Virgin Mary fashionably pale too, which is equally improbable if not more so.

The shop assistant wouldn't sell the icon to me as one of the patriarchs was in the church. Officially, they were only supposed to sell items of such a sacred nature to members of their congregation. I had to wait there for twenty-five minutes at the little store, till the coast was clear.

I took the bus back to the hostel where I was staying and everyone kept doing the trinity while I was sitting on the bus with the painting I got. It was really a freaky experience. Everywhere I went with the painting with the poem and the photo of Jesus, people kept signing the cross to themselves. Finally, with some relief, I got back to where I was staying and I rolled the painting up and sent it back to my massage therapist in New Zealand. I told her Romania was free now and I had enjoyed myself.

Romanian is a Romance language, related to Spanish and Italian, Portuguese and French. This comes as a surprise to many people since Romania is so far east. I could read the Latin letters and get myself around, which was great for going on the buses (I wasn't using Google Maps then). And knowing French helped to make things less unfamiliar, as well. I was amazed, and I was pleased to be there.

TRANSYLVANIA

I'd always loved *The Rocky Horror Picture Show*. There was a movie theatre in Avondale in Auckland that played it every weekend for years. I even met the musical's writer and creator Richard O'Brien, a New Zealand citizen and actor who played Riff Raff in the film.

As the lead character in the film, Doctor Frank N. Furter was the sweet transvestite from Transylvania. I decided to go there to experience the place, a large historical province in the inland northwest of Romania. It was only a five hour drive from Bucharest, so I set off.

Transylvania comes from *Transilvania* or 'beyond the forest' in Romanian, a name that suggests that the place was historically somewhat isolated and under-developed compared to other, more accessible parts of Europe.

Though part of Romania today, Transylvania was part of the Kingdom of Hungary for nearly all of its history prior to 1918 and was known to Hungarians as *Erdély*, which itself means 'the forest region'.

The Hungarian name finds its way into other languages, including Romanian. Thus the Romanians also call the region *Ardeal*, which sounds like some elf-inhabited fantasy kingdom in the writings of J. R. R. Tolkien, or perhaps C. S. Lewis's *The Lion, the Witch and the Wardrobe*. This is a beautiful name, which I prefer.

And Transylvania was colonised by many German-speaking settlers as well. In German the region is known as *Seibenbürgen*, 'Sevencastles', a reference not to castles as such (of which there are a lot more than seven in Transylvania), but to the seven historically German-speaking towns and cities it contained. A coat of arms showing an eagle watching over seven castles or towers, representing towns, was devised in the 1590s by a designer named Levinus Hulsius and soon adopted with additional modifications to reflect the presence of other populations.

Though Germans were mostly driven out of Eastern Europe after 1945 in retributive acts of ethnic cleansing, half a million were still present in

Transylvania in 1989. Virtually all then departed to Germany, leaving only about forty thousand today. A Transylvanian coat of arms based on Hulsius's design is still present as part of the modern-day Romanian coat of arms, along with coats of arms representing other regions.

Bran Castle, an honest-to-God castle, was something else. The former King and Queen of Romania had lived there in the 1920s but it's most

Initial version of the Transylvania coat of arms by Levinus Hulsius, said to be reproduced in his book Chronologia Rerum Memorabilium in Hungaria, Transilvania, &c., Gestatorum, Usque ad Annum 1597. *This image is from a public domain version of the Hulsius coat of arms, sourced from the Wikipedia entry on 'Historical coat of arms of Transylvania' on 12 November 2016; three blemishes were removed.*

famous for being (supposedly) the home of Dracula. Bran Castle is a spectacular elevated fortress built in the twelfth century, and then rebuilt a hundred years later to become the castle that stands there now.

It's not clear how it got to be known as Dracula's castle. The Irish novelist Bram Stoker, the author of the famous 1897 novel *Dracula*, never visited Bran castle nor apparently even knew of its existence. Vlad the Impaler, the notorious ruler who was also known as Dracula in his lifetime ('son of the dragon') and whose name was pinched by Stoker, was the tyrant of neighbouring Wallachia: Transylvania being part of Hungary at the time, of course.

Though it stood on the border with Wallachia, Bran Castle was a Hungarian border post for most of its history. It seems never to have anything to do with the real historical Dracula other than to look down on the Bran Gorge, through which he passed into Ardeal on several diplomatic journeys. Thus we must rescue Transylvania from some of the things that have been said about the place.

Transylvania is beyond Medieval—it feels like stepping back in time. Many villagers still favour horse-drawn carriages and carts over automobiles; it feels like you're wandering around a thousand years ago. And the landscape is spectacular. Beautifully-preserved castles and fortresses, around a hundred of them, decorate the soaring mountains and beautiful lakes and rivers: Ardeal, indeed, and henceforth.

If the current Māori name for New Zealand, Aotearoa, is an invented tradition in its most harmless sense — a highly poetical and uplifting name for a new nation, a name which may or may not have some connection to Kupe and his family assuming they ever existed, but which stands on its own merits as well — the identification of Transylvania with Dracula and vampires is an invented tradition in a worse sense.

All this Dracula stuff is the defamation of a charming and historical region via a collection of stories that seem to have little basis in any sort of fact whatsoever: the fictional Dracula an imaginary figure of course, and the real historical Dracula, though born in a Transylvanian town when his family were given sanctuary there, nonetheless the ruler of a neighbouring country and by and large an enemy of the Transylvanians as an adult.

Indeed, Transylvanian authors may have been responsible for exaggerating Vlad's cruelties as a form of literary revenge: another invented tradition, perhaps!

But with the end of my time in Transylvania — or Ardeal — it was time to leave Europe and head back to New Zealand to sort out the closure of my education business. Even though I'd already taken steps while overseas to shut operations down, I had to superintend the final stages in person.

Maree (right) and I, setting off to see the South Island before travelling overseas

Masters' graduation, 1993, with Brian Shackleton and my mother

Dad and I in Glenorchy recently, a Lord of the Rings *location*

*My mother's funeral programme, showing dad and the garden she
used to maintain: plus the angora goats mum used to breed
for their wool, used in the jacket shown*

*Leading the Hero Parade in Auckland, 1993: Myself while Auckland
City Councillor (left of photo), a third person in the middle and my
friend and activist Rosemary Segedin on the right.*

Graceland, where Elvis wrote his songs

The Alliance team in Mount Albert, Auckland. Myself as Auckland City Councillor in the middle of the front row, and Alliance Mount Albert Community Board members (from left) Syd Pilkington, Linda Cudby, Phil Amos, Chris Harris (Chair of Community Board), Gillian Dance and John Sanderson

New Orleans House of Blues and Voodoo

Getting face-painted in the Quechua style!

The Grand Canyon with James

Women preparing reeds on Lake Titicaca

Double-hulled reed boat on Lake Titicaca

Loved New Orleans and the Mardi Gras!

*Five-course dinner with Bernard and his family,
in a traditional dwelling in Corsica*

New York — and photo with NYPD and a fellow traveller from Germany

Belinda and I at the Colosseum

Marrakech

Versailles, in front of a representation of Louis XIV

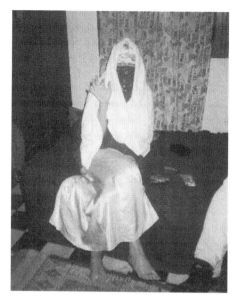

Dressed in the Moroccan style

Corsican road-sign, shot up and graffitied by separatists

Mary Jane in Corsica

CHAPTER TWENTY-SIX

Machu Picchu and a Famous Mummy

I wrapped up my business in New Zealand and went to look after my mother. She'd been through the wringer. Our family had hired a personal carer to look after her and he had stolen valuable possessions including my brother's motorbike; a Winchester rifle that was worked with a lever as in Westerns and fired blunt, old-fashioned-looking bullets; and, a well-crafted shotgun that fitted my father's shoulder like a glove.

I contacted the police but they seemed reluctant to put much time into the complaint, even though the guy in question was (as it turned out) already a known criminal and p-freak: the New Zealand idiom for someone who is a slave to crystallised methamphetamines, not the sort of person you should entrust with a shotgun, a cowboy rifle and a motorbike to ride off with both on the highway to Hell.

I then contacted the local MP in Thames, Sandra Goudie, now mayor of Thames, who was very supportive. Apparently this guy really was well-known for preying on elderly people to feed his habit. Sadly, despite Sandra's efforts and mine nothing was ever resolved.

The following year, 2009, I tried to get back into relief teaching. The recession had killed all the high-end employment companies and a lot of them became online-based. A lot of finance companies collapsed in New Zealand — fifty of them — and many people lost their life savings. In 2009 house values in Auckland went down by $80,000. They quickly bounced back, however, which just goes to show that Auckland is quite resilient in comparison to parts of Europe that have still not actually fully recovered from the crisis.

I'd developed a lot of back pain due to all the computer work that I do. I tried to have it diagnosed and was told it was wear and tear, and that I couldn't spend a lot of time in front of a computer ever again. Extreme sports and mountaineering become the solution in the end.

Accident Compensation Corporation (ACC) weren't coming to the party but luckily I had private health insurance and they gave me a pay-out. Now that I had an unexpected windfall of $11,000 I thought I would take the opportunity to change my posture and travel. Well my business wasn't making any money and I couldn't work. To this day I don't know why I have a sore back, I know part of it is emotional and part of it is bad posture.

A few months later I decided to go to South America. I'd developed a solid friendship with a Chilean man called Juan. He was a greenie and gay and we were very close.

Juan's father was a lawyer who had represented the former Chilean dictator, Augusto Pinochet. After taking power in a CIA-backed coup in 1973, Pinochet tortured, murdered and 'disappeared' tens of thousands of liberal Chileans and was eventually arrested for his crimes while visiting London in 1998. Although he was charged, he was never actually convicted of any wrongdoing and he returned to Chile in 2000 on medical grounds. He spent years under house arrest before dying of a heart attack in 2006.

South America has long had a political philosophy that was based on 'liberation theology', before the term itself was coined in South America in the 1960s by Gustavo Gutiérrez, a Peruvian theologian and Dominican priest.

Around the same time, an African liberation theology was happening in

South Africa. This continued due to the great need for social and political liberation among black people, and it became intertwined with the political struggles of the time.

In terms of the Americas as a whole, the original South Americans were believed to have been nomadic hunter- gatherers who migrated from Asia. Many empires were later established and were highly developed by 1000 BC, including the Cañaris culture of Ecuador, the Chimu Empire and the Chachapoya in Peru, and the Aymara kingdoms of Bolivia. After Columbus explored parts of South America and the Spanish invaded, the Inca Empire was wiped out due to a combination of superior weaponry and military tactics on the part of the Spanish and the corruption of the Inca leadership. However, their descendants and traditions still live on today.

In the 1500s, many places were invaded and precious commodities were discovered throughout South America. Silver was discovered in Bolivia, giving Spain immense wealth. Later on, of course, Bolivia would become independent.

Bolivia is one of the poorest South American countries despite still being abundant in mineral and energy resources, due to a long history of dictatorships, followed by huge indebtedness to the World Bank which demanded the mass privatisation in the 1980s of its resources and infrastructure.

Among the South American countries Bolivia has the largest proportion of indigenous people, who make up around two-thirds of the population.

When I went to South America, Ecuador had been given money by Hugo Chávez of Venezuela in order to be politically independent of the International Monetary Fund (IMF).

A number of the South American countries, such as Peru and Ecuador, are now governed by administrations dominated by the indigenous people, who are often opposed to mining and rampant industrial development of the fly-by-night variety — they're there to protect the environment. Bolivia even introduced a law, giving rights to 'mother earth' and its ecosystems, to protect the country's natural resources and people from exploitation.

The rise of anti-USA populists like Chávez can be traced to a history of US meddling in Latin America, none of it very creditable. The region was at one point very much like the modern day Middle East in terms of political instability and chronic United States interference, the two going hand in hand. This was during the Cold War in particular, when the USA got caught up in a vicious circle of supporting right-wing dictatorships because they were anti-Communist, whereupon the local land reformers and democrats, whom the North Americans should have been supporting, drifted toward the left and redoubled their revolutionary efforts — and so on and so forth. It was a pattern that could be seen from Mexico to Chile, via countries that were in the headlines for years such as Nicaragua.

Effectively the USA ended up on 'the wrong side of history' in Latin America. It was the same in South Africa, where the USA and Britain backed the Apartheid regime almost to the end against Nelson Mandela's African National Congress, which had to go to the Soviets for support. Nobody in the West likes to talk about that these days, and even Mandela himself was diplomatic enough not to rub it in after he was finally released and became president — and everybody's hero.

These days the USA seems to have quietly abandoned Latin America and left the locals to find their own path. One wonders if years from now we'll be saying something similar about an avoidable series of blunders in the Middle East...

I'd been raised as a Roman Catholic but in South America there is a different branch of Roman Catholicism. In Rome the church is conservative but it seems that the further away from Rome one gets the more freedom people have to alter their faith to suit their country and community. I was going to spend time with my friend Juan. Juan was raised as Opus Dei, which is a very conservative section of the Catholic Church. He'd been sexually abused by his uncle who was a priest (and into Opus Dei).

Juan was going to meet me in Santiago de Chile, the capital city of Chile, a city with a population of seven million. I stayed in the Historical District and was introduced to Juan's friends. One buddy James was a photographer and we went out to free brand clothing party launches. My photo even ended up in a local paper with Juan. I saw protest signs by the indigenous Mapuche people wanting liberation from Chile.

One night, we clubbed with one of Juan's friends who was a DJ and was off to Greece for a series of lucrative gigs. I boogied all night and I met this drug dealer selling ketamine (a horse tranquilizer) and realised that everyone around me was smoking crack! I didn't smoke crack! I went to bed at midnight and got up at 7am feeling quite refreshed. They'd stayed up all night. Juan and his friend James laughed at me. It was in a very upmarket part of Santiago and the woman who ran the place was very cultured, but I discovered I was locked in. I remember ringing my boyfriend at the time. "I'm locked into a crack party," I told him. He laughed.

Juan had a friend who was a member of the Freemasons and I find the presence of the Freemasons and their political allegiances very interesting. The Freemasons, or Masonic Order as they are otherwise known, belong to an organisation that was shaped in the fourteenth century around craft guilds. Some of them still have male members only.

Juan had warned me that his Freemason friend was addicted to drugs and was in the process of losing everything. There was a sense that something really horrible had happened to those people in Chile. People were very frightened of the far right and the military. Even so, they had just elected a socialist single mother, Michelle Bachelet, which was saying something for Chile. She served as president from 2006-10 and was elected again in 2014 with an even bigger majority.

Drugs are fast being decriminalised in South America, as they have been in Portugal. (It is perhaps no coincidence that the War on Drugs is the last great militarised intervention of the USA in Latin America: make drugs legal, and the War ends.) I agree with decriminalisation — it actually does work. I do realise the consequences of legalising drugs within society: there has to be a line somewhere. There have to be serious public health interventions to help addicts and regulation of sale and distribution, not just open slather.

If drugs were legal, I'd have my preferences and I do know what I would use. In 2008, party pills were legalized and I did try those. I made a decision when I was in South America that I wouldn't use cocaine because I didn't agree with it. Drugs can really destroy lives.

Anyway, the people at the crack party were otherwise cultured, wealthy and nice and I had a good friend around me, someone I knew I could trust, so it was OK. Things could have turned out worse.

We spent a lot of time out partying to 4am, not my idea of fun but it seemed ingrained in their way of life. I decided I'd had enough of partying. I found that drugs went hand in hand with parties there. That's why I wanted to stop partying because I don't like the drug scene, I'm fine with my own company and I'm fine not having my consciousness raised through drugs. The number of people in my friendship circle who can take drugs moderately is virtually non-existent. It's a shame really. I've only got one or two friends who can. Therefore, I choose not to participate.

As much as I enjoyed seeing Juan I had to move on.

The pollution and the partying were making me irritable. It was a bit like being in New Delhi: I mean the pollution was really, really bad.

I literally couldn't breathe sometimes.

The intercity coaches that I was to take in Chile were amazing. They had brand new first-class seating in that resembled pods in business class airlines, with individual TV screens. You could have sit-up seats or laid-back seats and they were relatively cheap, depending on the type of seat you bought.

There were toilets on board so bussing here was a pleasure, though it probably always pays to bring wipes just in case. I travelled about 1600km north from Santiago to San Pedro De Atacama. The journey took about eighteen hours.

I went to a place called Agua Fuentes and people were drinking tequila and playing cards in the street. There were fascinating older hacienda-type buildings, which was great.

I did four days of touring, some of which started at three in the morning to take advantages of particular phenomena. I saw beautiful geysers at El Tatio and desolate landscapes that looked like the moon. The most memorable tour was when I was in a vehicle like a jeep and we went very high, up to about 4,500 metres. I didn't know anything then about altitude mountain sickness. The guide said, "If you can't walk just lie down and breathe."

I had bought some cacao lollies, which you can use to combat altitude mountain sickness; they were meant to be natural remedies.

I went on all the Spanish-speaking tours because they were half the price of the English-speaking tours. It was one good way of getting to know the local people. I found that the French I'd picked up on the *Elf-Chine* and living in France meant that I could communicate with the people on these tours; many Spanish people speak French.

The tour guide had recently been left by his wife. He wanted me to be the mother of his children and look after his daughter. As flattered as I was I couldn't see myself living there with him. It was wonderful there though. I saw flamingos even though it rarely rains; maybe once every hundred years.

This condition mainly results from the Humboldt or Peru Current, a cold current that flows northward from Antarctic regions up the west coast of South America, over a deep trench that lies just offshore. The current is at its strongest where the northern end of Chile meets Peru, where the angle of the coast concentrates the current. In this area, the rate of evaporation of the cold, upwelling seawater is too feeble to combat the heat of the tropical sun. Clouds and fog form, but save for once every hundred years or so, there is not enough moisture in the air to actually form rain.

The *quid pro quo* is that the cold, upwelling water supports a wonderful fishery and an abundance of marine life in general, in the same way that it does at Kaikoura in New Zealand; but on a vaster scale since we are talking about South America, not little old New Zealand.

The Chilean government had moved a glacier for mining. The glaciers are hugely important for the farmers in the Huasco Valley, who depend on the run-off water. The reckless relocation of large chunks of glacier has threatened this delicate balance. During my bus trip to San Pedro de Atacama I didn't know which piles of rock were tailing heaps from the mines, and which piles were natural hills. It was that confusing and quite sad. A lot of the miners weren't paid very well at all, to find copper and lithium in the mines.

Mountain people here dress exactly the same as the Nepalese; similar designs and styles of clothing — thick tapestry overskirts with black hats and long braids. I found it fascinating!

PERU

The border crossing here can be tricky, but I didn't have any problems because I was travelling with three other people. I'd heard that being alone at a border crossing can result in getting bribery-type fines to let you through. And I didn't want to be stuck at the mercy of a border crossing guard! I stopped in at Lake Titicaca where you can see the neighbouring countries and visit a sustainable floating village. The people living there, the Uru, live on floating reeds. Their boats are floating reeds. Their houses are floating reeds.

I found out later on Māori Television that similar canoes made out of reeds were used by Māori in New Zealand. A Māori tribe went over to Lake Titicaca and saw the canoes, and said that they were a part of their whakapapa (genealogy).

While it is tempting to suppose that there must have been a connection, the notion is undermined by the fact that the ancient Egyptians made boats out of floating reeds as well. If anyone were to claim a strong connection between New Zealand Māori, indigenous South Americans and ancient Egyptians based on the use of reed boats, that theory would be dismissed by most people as flakey. It is literally one step too far. Two is believable, three is a crowd.

More likely, each culture independently devised the reed boat. Or perhaps they were all descended from some very distant common ancestors who knew about various means of making rafts and boats, in the same way that every culture on earth seems to know about fire and axes.

Even so, it has often been claimed with a reasonable degree of seriousness that there *might be* a South American connection to New Zealand, or to Polynesia in general, all the same.

The established view of the origins of the Polynesians, and of the Māori as a subgroup of Polynesians — a view backed up by masses of evidence from multiple sources — is that Polynesia was settled from the West, from Asia and its offshore islands including the islands of Melanesia, and that this is where all the primary cultural and genetic influences came from. Toward the end of this process some Eastern Polynesians then doubled back on a more southerly track and discovered New Zealand. Such is the well-attested orthodoxy.

Even so, it is at least conceivable that some Polynesian seafarers got all the way to South America, and that there was some secondary influence in the other direction, obscured by the primary influence in the same way that the moon is easily missed on those occasions when it appears in the daytime.

In 1947 the explorer Thor Heyerdahl and his colleagues floated a raft, the *Kon-Tiki*, westward from South America to the heart of Polynesia to show that it could be done. And the easternmost site of a confirmed Polynesian culture, Rapa Nui or Easter Island, is sufficiently far east to be nowadays part of Chile. One or two recent scientific studies of DNA also support the idea of some contact.

Perhaps future advances in DNA analysis and other sciences will provide a more definite answer as to how much interaction there really was between Polynesia and South America.

On the way to Lima I dropped into Miraflores, a lovely coastal town. I was meeting tourists who seemed to be addicted to cocaine everywhere. Peru was a magnet for white coke fiends. It was boring, because they're strange. These people were openly having sex in the mixed dorm. From then on I only stayed in female dorms.

Lima was an experience. I was just walking around and I met this guy who wanted to practise his French because he'd lived in France. I thought that even though I was supposed to be speaking Spanish I was spending more time speaking French, because everyone on the tour was speaking it here. He gave me a guided tour of Lima, mostly from a French perspective: the Napoleon Bonaparte French military barracks and a small replica of the Statue of Liberty in the New York Casino. I stayed about three days then headed to north to begin what was to be a nightmarish guided tour.

CUZCO

Everyone was sniffing at the hostel. They told me they had colds so I spent the first morning running around making tea for everyone. It turned out their blocked noses weren't related to the flu at all — I've just explained the real reason!

I started talking to an Irish girl at the hostel bar and she said that she was in trouble because she had to be a drug mule. She and a group of people were making their way up to Colombia with the drugs to send them somewhere (to Europe I think).

Alcohol consumption gets out of control and so travellers just freely try whatever other drug is offered to them. The drugs there were being supplied by the barman, but her cocaine habit had gone up to $2700 so she was being stalked by people, locals and taxi drivers, to pay them back.

I was worried. "Look, if you really want to get out of this mess, I'd be quite prepared at 5am to take you to the Irish embassy. But you've got to get yourself out of this mess. You've got to get on a bus and get out of here."

She looked at me and said, "I can't do it. Shall we go out dancing tonight?" That's when I realised that I was not going to go out in that town. And I wasn't going to spend any more time with that silly person. She was supposedly an educated woman in her thirties, a former primary school teacher. It was tragic.

In the 1400s Cuzco was the capital of the Inca Empire. Now its claim to fame is that it's the gateway to the Sacred Valley of the Incas and Machu Picchu.

I still have my ticket for Machu Picchu. I love the overall ethos of the design. They didn't use nails and some stone buildings are constructed without mortar — they just fitted in with each other. They had different agricultural areas where they grew certain types of fruits and trees at different altitudes, with a unique system of horticulture. It was such an advanced culture. They had natural sewerage system and fountains where every two minutes the irrigation system worked, sustainably.

It's a spectacular sight; ancient stone stairs and tiered castle-type ruins disappearing high into the mountains. Only discovered a hundred years ago by an American history lecturer hiking alone through the Andes, or rediscovered I suppose you could say, Machu Picchu has become a standard item on bucket lists. More than a million people come here each year to see the estate complete with temples, residences that the inhabitants of the Inca civilisation built for their emperor in 1450. Its remote location saved it from being destroyed during the Spanish Conquest in 1532.

I climbed up and started crying because I was overwhelmed by being so high in the sky! I had to stop and deliberately chill out in a yoga fashion. I was feeling anxious and the guide looked a little bit drunk to me.

"What's wrong with your eyes?" I asked him. "Are you on cocaine?" "No, I'm on iowaska."

I didn't know at that stage what it was, but later on I discovered it was a hallucinogenic tea that also went by the name ayahuasca. Ayahuasca is the Spanish spelling and in indigenous languages it is also spelt iowaska or ayawaska; the pronunciation is much the same.

Machu Picchu was packed. I think damage was being done to the site because there were so many people. There was talk that they were going to rope the area off and this was the last opportunity to get there.

I went to the Santa Catalina Monastery and was interested to discover how human-like qualities in churches are revered here. Many believe that the statues actually cry. They certainly looked alive.

On a tour bus to Puerto Malabrigo I was the odd one out. Of the twenty-five people on the bus I was the only one not singing high school musical songs. Everyone else was fresh out of high school and on a gap year. It wasn't working for me.

An elderly Swiss guy on the bus was taking photos with an old-fashioned camera that looked like it was forty years old. The young group made fun of him and completely ostracised him. At the end of the tour all the younger people wanted to do was eat pizza and pasta. They were boring. I wanted to go to hear some Quechua folk music. Obviously I wasn't going to last long with them.

In Puerto Malabrigo I met a shaman/hostel owner. He was aloof and hooked on cocaine, snorting it left right and centre, unashamedly hoovering up white lines. I didn't know what to think at that point but the other people I met here were very friendly; the taxi driver took a shine to me and invited me to his family home by the beach. I was surprised to see the same sorts of trees being planted here that I have at home. *Ficus Benjamina* need a lot of work; they have to be trimmed extensively and their roots need cutting every two years. My uncle had these trees in Brisbane. They can grow under the foundations of a house and can disrupt everything from plumbing to electrical wiring.

The taxi driver listened to my concerns about these particular trees being planted less than a metre from the boundary of his house. He told his next-door neighbour that I knew about trees and that they were inappropriate to plant there. From then on I was treated like a queen; he became my personal driver.

Even though my mini personal tour was fantastic, the group tour was awful! All the students and younger people were binge drinking, I don't think there was a moment they weren't hammered. They were rude to everyone over thirty and ended up in a massive brawl with another tour group.

The tour guide was a young guy from the United States. The guy asked me if I would have sex with him and he would give me cocaine. I of course declined.

When we got to the border between Peru and Ecuador he didn't have a visa. And then we ran out of petrol. I was over it.

ECUADOR

After finally crossing the border into southern Ecuador our first stop was a famous Panama hat factory in Cuenca called Homero Ortega. And it's where I left the tour. I just couldn't spend time around these people anymore. I asked for a refund. They refused. I elevated my complaint to the Australian-based tour company, which expressed concern that if I left the tour I'd be alone in a dangerous country.

I told them, "I'm safer by myself, the only thing that is dangerous are the people I'm touring with. The binge-drinking culture, the cocaine snorting."

I'd been terrorized by the media's attempts to convince everyone that South America's dangerous. I was extremely careful. I wasn't going to go out in a dark alley by myself at night. I was always going to make sure I knew where I was going, and made sure I wasn't going to arrive anywhere at night. I wouldn't even walk around my own town, Queenstown, late at night. I think you've just got to apply those rules, don't be drunk, don't be stoned and don't be stupid. I'd rather do my own tours.

I went to Guayaquil in Ecuador, which, although a sprawling city, was close to the beautiful Machalilla National Park. I hired a guide and I trekked through the park alongside the South Pacific Ocean. It reminded me of the area in and around the port hills of Christchurch with the big brown grasses, except they had bizarre-looking bromeliads. I fell in love with the contrasted foliage.

After there I went to Quito and I hired a guide to go up into the hills. While pretty villagers were painting my face I asked the guide whether his son spoke Quechua.

"No," he told me.

"Why not?"

He sort of looked at me and didn't really know why. It's because Quechua, once the official language of the Inca Empire, was destroyed by the Spanish four hundred years ago and now, though it's still spoken by a quarter of the population, it's dying out. The major problem with the survival of the language is the lack of reading material available in it. It's largely a spoken language these days.

He was a fantastic guide and at only $21 per day he was great value for money. One of the local villages he took me to made their living selling macaw parrots as hats, quite sad!

Because I trusted whom I was with, I decided to get some iowaska, the hallucinogenic drug I'd become aware of at Machu Picchu. Technically iowaska is an entheogen, meaning that the main content of the trip is feeling spiritual.

Iowaska does not agree with everyone and you might get chronic diarrhoea and vomit among various other unpleasant side effects, including the possibility of a bad trip: so I only took an eighth of the recommended dose. I sort of hallucinated. I heard everything in the jungle but never really saw anything. I imagine if I'd taken what I was supposed to I would have had an intense trip. But being on drugs in the jungle could have got strange very quickly, so I was glad I was sensible.

I spent three days in a thatched tree-house three metres high off the ground; exploring the local wildlife. There was bat shit everywhere (which tells you how many bats are in the rainforest!).

After three days in the jungle I headed back to Quito and was warned by the hostel's owner not to go out at night. But after years of travelling I'm pretty savvy when I'm in another country. I don't wear expensive jewellery or walk around holding an iPhone. I wear plain clothes and no make-up. I look like a *traveller* and not a tourist.

The churches were beautiful with statues of the saints, including Mariana de Jesus de Paredes, a patron saint of Quito. In Ecuador the currency was the US dollar (though the president was very anti-USA).

GALAPAGOS

Tours to the Galapagos Islands are a heck of a lot cheaper to buy from Quito but they're still expensive. For $3900 I took a four-day trip on a former pirate ship to the islands of Santa Cruz, Fernandina and Isabella, all of which sit in across the equator in the Pacific Ocean.

The Galapagos Islands are famous for their giant tortoises and of course being the place where Charles Darwin studied and developed the theories of evolution and natural selection.

Everyone on the boat was in their twenties and wanted to go diving to view hammerhead sharks. You've got to be kidding me! I was not interested. Māori have a saying 'don't die like the octopus, die like the hammerhead shark'. Sharks have a reputation for being dangerous both in the water and when 'safely' landed in a boat. But hammerheads, it seems, can be particularly combative.

I didn't mind swimming with seals in murky water, even though one got a little too close and aggressive. But there was no way I was going to get up close and personal with sharks. The only shark I want to see is on my dinner plate!

Everyone on the boat asked how old I was and because I thought it was none of their business they just assumed I was ancient. I made friends with the only other comparably-aged person on the boat, a Greek guy called Iki who also didn't want to get into the shark-infested waters. During the Greek financial crisis he lost his job, his teeth and had to move back to family land to grow food.

I was surprised by the physical appearance of the islands; because I'd seen images of tree-covered islands I wasn't expecting to see so much volcanic rock. They looked more like a moonscape rather than a tropical island.

I enjoyed the Galapagos Islands, the flightless shag, the rainbow-coloured iguanas, bright red and orange crabs and Lonesome George the celibate hundred year-old tortoise and the last surviving member of the Pinta Island Tortoise subspecies. His subsequent death in 2012 means that I was one of the last people to see him, and to see that particular subspecies. Sad.

ARGENTINA

I've always wanted to go to Buenos Aires, the capital of Argentina, mostly because of my possibly uncritical admiration for the glamour of Eva Perón and the Perón dynasty.

Eva was a heroine for the masses, not only for being the exceptionally beautiful wife of popular president Juan Perón, but because she came from humble beginnings and was committed to charity. Their politics were on the fence. They weren't communists and they weren't capitalists, which is probably why they were both so popular across the board.

After her death at the age of thirty-three in 1952, Eva was embalmed in a process that took over two years and cost over $80,000. The reason it took so long was that her body was ravaged by cancer so there was a lot of painstaking work to complete before she could lie in state for eternity. Every single drop of her fluids had to be replaced with wax to preserve her internal organs and physical appearance.

Even after her husband was overthrown in a coup she was still kept in immaculate condition. At one point she was apparently smuggled to Italy (how they got a famous corpse out of a country was amazing) but she eventually returned to her husband and 'lived' in their house together with him and his new wife Isabel on a specially built platform in the dining room.

It's one thing to have exes hanging around but to have a mummified ex watching you eat dinner? Creepy! At least she was still looking good; I guess she'd never age past 33.

In 1974 when Juan Perón was back in power after an 18-year break in exile, he commissioned a team of experts to "restore" her. Apparently she'd suffered a bit of damage over the years, which is not surprising given the numerous smugglings and kidnappings.

The Eva Perón museum was astounding; it was like going back in time. The display scenes around her are also from the 1950s — her clothing, the furniture and artwork are a snapshot of what life was like when she was the First Lady.

I loved Argentina. The music was everywhere. Street musicians brought the place to life and the food was incredible: lots of barbecued meat flavoured with Chimichurri, a sauce made from herbs, garlic and vinegar. Divine.

Sadly I ran out of time. And I had to get to the Caribbean!

ST MARTIN

10 hours north of Buenos Aires is the island of St Martin, a Caribbean paradise known for being the place that the rich and famous holiday. I was going to see Mary whom I'd met on the Chinese junk, *Elf-Chine*, her son and her new beau Jacques.

I can see why it's so popular with the jet-set; breath-taking white sand beaches straight out of a postcard and, as it's only a three hour flight from America and has an abundance of luxury accommodation and experiences, it's a perfect getaway. Cheaper holidays are available there though: you can pick up all-inclusive packages in the States for a reasonable price.

The island is divided in two, oddly so for such a small place. The northern part is French and the southern belongs to the Netherlands.

In 1648 the current governing nations kicked the Spanish out and divided it for themselves. Even though there are two predominant languages, depending on where you are on the island, English is spoken everywhere. The slave trade was huge here; people were forced to work on sugar plantations and subjected to unimaginable cruelty. Unsurprisingly there were countless uprisings and rebellions. Eventually the French abolished slavery in 1848. The Dutch were a little slower to recognise basic human rights, making slavery illegal fifteen years later in 1863. But it still took a further two years for the American government to ban slavery (and almost another hundred years for segregation to be made unlawful). Shocking.

The Caribbean has a long history of European colonization — before most of Latin America — and has been the slowest to claim its independence. With the obvious and ambiguous exception of Cuba, even those countries that did gain their independence continue to be slaves to globalization to varying degrees.

The French put a lot of money into St Martin, and there's free healthcare. Mary told me that the Creole people, the majority inhabitants of the French part, want independence from the French but they also want their funding. Having both isn't possible, obviously. But she also told me that the French doctors there look after everyone, even if you're a penniless overstayer.

There's a huge crack problem on the island. Sweet Mary believed that drug dealers standing around at the end of the street were just waiting for their friends who were running late — bless her.

I went to a wedding while I was in St Martin, and that was a good experience. He was a French guy and she was a Romanian woman, they were both lovely! At their wedding there was loads of French paté and Romanian salami. I am not a fan of either, so I ended up eating peanuts the whole day!

I had brought what I thought were really nice bottles of wine from New Zealand. Mary was cooking from home and feeding French doctors and offered them my wine, and they said, "Oh we don't like nouveau Beaujolais."

A little miffed I returned to New Zealand where "new" wine is appreciated!

CHAPTER TWENTY-SEVEN
The Arctic Circle

I went to Iceland on a whim; I'd discovered that they'd jailed the perpetrators of the economic collapse in 2008 and told the International Monetary Fund (IMF) to get stuffed when it proposed some kind of austerity programme. These were my kind of people!

Iceland is a little less than half the size of New Zealand but has well under a tenth of New Zealand's population. It's easy to feel lost in the remoteness of it all. The word Iceland comes to us from the local name *Ísland*, which actually does mean land of ice, and not island or 'the island' as one might have thought! The word refers to Iceland's many glaciers, though these glaciers do not cover the whole country or even most of it.

Indeed, in spite of a far northerly latitude, almost on the Arctic Circle, there is a low-lying region along the coast of Iceland which is surprisingly mild and temperate even in winter, thanks to a warm offshoot from the Gulf Stream called the Irminger Current. The climate in the temperate coastal strip is only a few degrees cooler, in summer and winter alike, than the southernmost tip of New Zealand, Stewart Island; which lies much closer to the equator, straddling latitude 47 degrees South, as opposed to lying mostly between 64 and 67 degrees North as Iceland does.

In fact just about all of the inhabitants of Iceland live in the temperate coastal strip. It is the small size of the overall temperate zone that accounts for Iceland's small population. It is not as if the population is spread all over the island, much of which is quite desolate.

Along with Stewart Island, something of a parallel could also be made with the South Island of New Zealand, which is about the size of Iceland (a little bigger); has a population of just a million, almost all of it tightly hugging the coast; and is also quite desolate and barren and even glaciated in much of the interior. Iceland is like the South Island of New Zealand — only more so.

As an island, Iceland is unusual in the sense that it is not a broken-off fragment of a continent or the higher part of a drowned continent, as New Zealand is; nor a volcano like many Pacific islands; nor the peak of a submerged hill like many coastal islands — but actually a raised-up section of true oceanic seafloor. Iceland is part of the spreading mid-Atlantic ridge, and giant cracks and fissures run through the landscape just as they do in the parts of the mid-ocean floor that are below the waves.

The population is made up of a mixture of descendents of Norwegian and Gaelic-speaking settlers with little or no presence from other groups such as the Inuit (the situation is quite different in Greenland). The Icelandic government runs on a Nordic social model, where healthcare and education even to tertiary level is either free, or low-cost.

I arrived on a Sunday and thought that the best way to meet the locals would be in a church. I was surprised at the simplicity of the church, of the Lutheran branch of Christianity. The exterior was minimal and modest and the interior lacked the lavishness of other churches I'd seen.

Iceland was quite an experience, from volcanic snowstorms that smashed in my car window to camping in sub-zero temperatures. This was a trip I would never forget.

GREENLAND

I'd planned to stay on the world's largest island apart from Australia, which is regarded as a continent, for a month. I wanted to take my time and really get to understand the country, the people and the culture. It's nearly ten times larger than New Zealand but has a total population of less than sixty thousand people, so it's even more sparsely settled than Iceland, which at that point had been the most under- populated country I'd visited. Despite the lack of people they have more than enough languages. West Greenlandic is the official language, which all children learn in addition to Danish and English. Greenlandic is an Inuit language. There are three other Greenlandic languages widely spoken: South Greenlandic, East Greenlandic and the Thule dialect.

The capital, Nuuk, has a population of sixteen and a half thousand — a respectable-sized town. For anyone who might have been expecting to find something like Scott Base in Antarctica, Nuuk is a lot bigger and more of a real town.

Even for me, an experienced traveller, it was a huge culture shock arriving in Nuuk. I was struck instantly by the overwhelming level of poverty and homelessness. It was surprising. And saddening. I felt that there was a lack of appreciation and recognition for the indigenous people, the Greenlandic Inuit. But then that's not an uncommon feeling I've picked up travelling the world.

Nuuk is only a few kilometres north of the Icelandic capital of Reykjavík, for of course Iceland itself is practically on the Arctic circle. T he most densely inhabited part of Greenland, using the word 'densely' in a relative sense, lies on exactly the same latitude as Iceland.

Even so, Greenland seems to be an incomparably harsher and more marginal place in which to live, because the influence of the Gulf Stream, which transports heat from the tropics to the North Atlantic, is weaker. Greenland is further west, closer to the notoriously frigid north-east coast of Canada, past which the icebergs slither in the cold Labrador Current, which flows in the opposite direction to the Gulf Stream.

Sub-Arctic is probably the best description of Nuuk, and of the other parts of Greenland that have significant populations. Nuuk never gets really incredibly cold in the true Arctic or Antarctic sense. But on the other hand it never seems to get above seven degrees Celsius either, even in high summer.

So, you can forget about luxuriant crops, the name 'Greenland' notwithstanding! A bit of tough grass is about as good as it gets, agriculture-wise, in those parts.

The Norse tried colonising Greenland in the Middle Ages, when the climate in the North Atlantic was in fact warmer than now due to the fact that the Gulf Stream was stronger than today.

That was when the paradoxical name Greenland was bestowed. The origin of the name is contested; some say that it was designed to make the place sound more appealing, in the same way that the promoter of a new suburb in modern times might call it Sunnyvale or Fruitvale. Another theory is that the 'Green' is a mistranslation of a word that originally meant 'Ground' or solid ground, a reference to its immensity perhaps.

Sadly, the first Greenland colony did not survive the natural cooling of the North Atlantic climate, the 'Little Ice Age', which took hold after the year 1300 and so famously led to ice-skating fairs on the River Thames in London, along with starvation, poverty, wars, plagues and witch-burning crazes as the crops failed in Europe and people looked for scapegoats.

The calamity of the Little Ice Age seems to have been caused by a weakening of the Gulf Stream, much as in the film *The Day After Tomorrow* (which was of course hugely exaggerated but based on a small kernel of fact). The Icelanders had it tough too, but survived. So, Iceland had the more off-putting name but turned out to be more habitable long-term; whereas Greenland was, and remains, right on the margin.

What amazed me was the large number of foreigners I met living in Greenland. They'd fallen in love with the harsh environment and had given up life in their homelands to live a quieter and colder existence. It was a bit like *Northern Exposure*, the fictional 1990s TV series about refugees from civilisation in Alaska. Except of course that the inhabited parts of Alaska are mostly pretty balmy compared to the inhabited parts of Greenland. I wouldn't live any further north than Nuuk without indoor plumbing, put it that way.

After my initial shock over the homelessness and poverty in a remote town with few industries and no agricultural hinterland, I fell in love with Greenland and its people all the same.

My month here was stunning. I met dozens of incredible people including an Inuit chief, and saw icebergs, glaciers, seals, Viking settlements from the old defunct colony, and went dog sledding. The climate in Greenland continues to change, nowadays as a result of global warming, which stands to improve the prospects for eventually being able to sunbathe in Nuuk, but which is also melting the wider Arctic in ways that are frankly disastrous along with disastrous implications elsewhere.

The impact of natural Gulf Stream fluctuations in the past, as disruptive as they were, was much more local and limited than global warming today. And of course the one percent kernel of truth in *The Day After Tomorrow* is also that global warming could indeed lead to a paradoxical return of Little Ice Age conditions, due to a southward spread of cold, fresh water from recently-melted glaciers and polar ice over the surface of the North Atlantic.

In Greenland

This would bring coldness normally locked up in the polar latitudes to points further south — scientists call it 'leaving the fridge door open' — and suppress the Gulf Stream as well, thus amplifying the effect. Some say that there is evidence for such a shift already, in terms of more harsh winters in Europe and North America of late. Of course the scientists are not talking about anything as over-the-top as in the movie, but it is still a concern.

My time with the Inuit and learning about the very real (and complicated) impacts of global warming, on top of unrelenting natural fluctuations that already made life difficult for people in the north, blew my mind!

To read more about my icy adventures in Iceland and Greenland, check out *A Maverick Inuit Way and the Vikings.*

Dog Sledding in Greenland

In Iceland

CHAPTER TWENTY-EIGHT
The Year I Decided to Run Away. Again.

I love tramping. And because I wanted to hang around like-minded people who enjoyed the same outdoor pursuits, in 2010 I joined the Auckland Tramping Club. Tramping is the New Zealand term for what is known in Britain as hiking, a form of outdoor recreation that gained mass popularity in the 1920s and 1930s as rural bus services penetrated rugged parts of the country for the first time, and as more and more people began to acquire personal automobiles and an interest in the outdoors as well. Because New Zealand is so mountainous and scenic, tramping has long been especially popular.

I spent two years as the Social Secretary but resigned due to irreconcilable differences, namely the general racism, right-wing behaviour and sexism that in my opinion permeates many tramping clubs around New Zealand. I know many people that have had similar experiences with tramping clubs and we all firmly believe that they'll die out unless they get with the times.

In the 1920s and 1930s, when they first became popular as in other countries, tramping clubs in New Zealand had rotating committees so everyone had the ability to take responsibility; there were no dominant personalities (or dictatorships). Membership seemed more inclusive unlike the elitist membership that exists today. In the Auckland Tramping Club's 2015 annual report they noted that membership was declining except for in the over-65 age group. They made special mention that they needed to attract younger members and were finding it a challenge. This wasn't of any surprise to me.

When the Auckland Tramping Club formed in 1925 their objectives were to encourage social interaction between members, encourage healthy pursuits and arrange outings throughout the Auckland region. And even though they banned women from the inaugural meeting in the volcanic cone on Rangitoto Island, they eventually relented. But sexism is still present, nearly 100 years later.

Unfortunately popular outdoor recreation and the sporting life in general has always had a tendency to attract a right-wing, semi-fascist element convinced that modern civilisation has made people go soft. And on top of that there is also a natural tendency for the spirit of groups of trampers to evolve in a Spartan and masochistic direction of athletic seriousness, of a head-down, tails-up, why-can't-you-keep-up mentality. The challenge is to find a way of enjoying such outdoor recreation minus the masochism or, as it would sometimes humorously be put, the element of 'salvation through suffering'.

Meetup groups were begun as an alternative to tramping clubs in 2003 by a group of people keen to create a sense of community and bringing people together. They currently have more than 10,000 members, a figure considerably more impressive than the 455 members that the Auckland Tramping Club has, as of the time of writing.

Tramping with Meetups was much more pleasurable; we were allowed to stop and take photos and encouraged to laugh and joke. I found that the organisers of the Meetup groups had a real passion for tramping in the sense of happy, social excursions.

* * *

Some time ago I'd planted seventy native trees on my property and as they grew into a beautiful subtropical forest it inspired me to experience more of the wild. And what better place to discover it than Auckland's Waitakere Ranges, a sixteen-thousand hectare park with 250 kilometres of tramping tracks, stunning views and prehistoric-looking forest vistas.

The area quickly became my training ground. The Paraha Valley near Whatipu was good for rock climbing, and the area behind Bethell's Beach was good for mud, mud, and more mud. My explorations took me to the east coast of the Auckland region too. I went to Shakespear Park and Anchor Bay, which were both great for learning how to scramble over larger rocks. Rangitoto Island was perfect for getting to grips with sharper volcanic rock. In Auckland we really have it all but even with all that variety on my doorstep I became footloose.

After only five months as a member of the Auckland Tramping Club, I went to the South Island to complete an eight-day tramp on the St James Walkway in North Canterbury, a name that puts one in mind of the famous pilgrim route in northern Spain also named after St James! We slept in tents and spent two days on the Harper Pass. That trip changed my view of life and was the catalyst for my love affair with the South Island in general. Little did I know that I would be living in Queenstown within eighteen months.

One member of the group wanted to do a fifteen-hour day (clearly a bid for salvation through suffering). I also found that some of the people in the club were opposed to New Zealand's Treaty of Waitangi and were very racist.

The first day on the St James Walkway it rained heavily, cutting off all road access to Christchurch and the West Coast and closing both ends of the Lewis Pass Road. What had been streams the night before were now torrents of water and rolling rock. It was impossible for us to cross. I'm an unabashed lover of hot pools and after I had worked hard to convince the more hard-core trampers of the group, we called it quits and went to the hotel and hot pool complex at Maruia Springs until things blew over.

There were eight of us in the St James Walkway group: a couple of other laid-back kiwis and myself, the leader who was a flexible kiwi bloke, a Hungarian hard-core tramper who bred geckos, a female cello player, a caregiver, and a head librarian. It was a group of mixed people, of mixed

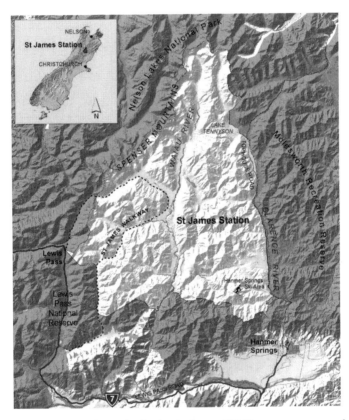

St James Station, after which the St James Walkway was named, was acquired by the New Zealand Government in 2008 and incorporated into a wider St James Conservation Area (DOC graphics, from 2008 press release, https://www.beehive.govt.nz/node/34954)

ages. Together we completed the entire Lake Daniell Walkway, bush-whacked up to the peaks and tarns — a 'tarn' is a small lake without visible streams flowing into it, common in the mountains — and then did the Harper Pass. Just as in a Victorian workhouse, some days were a full twelve hours of tramping.

In the end I went on strike and said I would do ten hours a day at the most.

The most memorable parts of the trip were the five a.m. gales on the Lewis Tops Track where we spent the night. I remember packing up in twenty minutes and then running down the hill, almost being blown over in the process. It was great having an adventure with nutty comrades in arms who all considered the experience to be completely normal. Like me, one other member of the group wanted to stay and live in the South Island.

The St James Walkway trip helped me understand how many of the more laid-back members of the Auckland Tramping Club do not take part in the longer trips. This is because they get bullied and sidelined by the more experienced members, who are known to dominate and cause conflict on the trips.

In September of 2012, when I was still organising speakers for the Auckland Tramping Club remotely from Queenstown, I was denied the opportunity to take part in a Dusky Sound trip and a tramp on Stewart Island. At this point, I resigned from the club in disgust.

Astonishingly, younger females are generally not allowed on Auckland Tramping Club trips unless they are married or are with the men who are also taking part in the trips. I found this situation to be quite archaic. Of course it's not officially in the club's policy: but many other single women have confirmed that it was pervasive, and didn't just happen to me. So much for joining a tramping club to try and meet up with people!

Thus is an ageing membership explained. Even so, the criticism does not seem to be welcome. When I tried to re-join in 2014 my membership was rejected: the first in seventy years to be vetoed. I was shocked.

DEPARTMENT OF CONSERVATION VOLUNTEERING

There were some positives to come out of my time with Auckland Tramping Club. One female member of the club changed my life forever by suggesting I become a Department of Conservation volunteer hut warden at Welcome Flat on the West Coast, the site of a famous hot pool. As soon as she suggested it, I was struck by the idea.

Not long after this suggestion I completed the Routeburn Track with friends and was extremely moved by the scenery. I truly could not believe such beauty existed but I was also annoyed it had taken me so long to realize that it did! While on this walk I met some dedicated hut wardens. Little did I know I would never be able to settle in Auckland permanently ever again.

ARROWTOWN

After a review of my businesses I decided I would be able to operate them remotely, leaving me free to pursue my plan of living one month in Arrowtown, then one month in Wanaka, to see if small town life in the South Island would suit me. Arrowtown was beautiful. With its heavy snow and frozen rivers it looked like a village from a fairy tale book. In these cooler, more southerly parts of New Zealand, deciduous European trees are often more commonly encountered in towns and cities than the evergreen native vegetation, much of it tropical in appearance even though the climate of New Zealand is similar to Europe.

Generally speaking the New Zealand 'bush', meaning forest, is divided into rain forest, which looks tropical or primeval, and beech forest. Only the beech forest would have looked familiar to pioneers. And even this was evergreen, unlike the beech forests back home.

Many of the early colonists suffered from homesickness. Evergreen vegetation, often strange in appearance, muted the familiar cycle of the seasons and made homesickness worse. To make matters worse there were very few conspicuous flowering plants: generally only small white flowers, fertilised by what seemed to be colour-blind bees. The four seasons were green, green, green and green, with little or no winter snow in much of the country, and no riot of colours in spring and autumn either. The alienating effect of the New Zealand bush was a very frequent complaint among the first settlers.

At first glance it might seem strange that New Zealand, a country with a climate similar to several of the countries of the North Atlantic, should be covered in so many areas by what looks like jungle. The reason for this is the 'oceanic' character of New Zealand and indeed the temperate zone of the southern hemisphere as a whole: a combination of mild winters, continual rainfall, and an absence of larger continental landmasses in the temperate zone of the Southern Hemisphere (most of Australia and Africa and South America are actually in the hot zone).

In the temperate part of the Southern Hemisphere, great deciduous forests like those of Asia, America and Europe did not evolve or become the dominant kind of foliage, with the exception of the southern beech forests of the genus Nothofagus which are deciduous in South America (though not in New Zealand). In Australia, where rainfall is unpredictable, eucalyptus forests became widespread, and there are also dryland plants in South Africa.

But otherwise, especially in New Zealand, evergreen tropical rainforests became surprisingly widespread: especially in coastal areas where forests of palms and creepers and all kinds of lush vegetation could be sure of escaping dry summer heat and freezing winters. It was true that the climate was often cool in New Zealand. But the nearby ocean, though unwarmed by any equivalent of the Gulf Stream, was still warm enough in New Zealand's latitudes to make sure that the air at sea level never dipped far below freezing. With the regular rain that the seas around New Zealand also brought, tropical jungles could adapt to a cool climate by simply growing more slowly.

The treeline in New Zealand is also surprisingly low, of the order of a thousand to fifteen hundred metres over most of the country, and just a few hundred metres on Stewart Island in the very south. Even on a fairly short uphill tramp, or a very short one on Stewart Island, we find that the trees get stumpier and more gnarled till we find ourselves in a sort of tundra, colloquially known as 'the tops'. In contrast the treeline can be well over three and a half thousand metres in the Rocky Mountains, at comparable latitudes to New Zealand.

The low treeline in New Zealand seems due to a combination of an absence of continental summertime heating of the landscape; strong winds and intense rainfall on New Zealand's tops; and the lack of cold-hardiness of many New Zealand tree species. A major ecological problem in New Zealand is the invasion of local pseudo-tundra by Northern Hemisphere species of tree, pines in particular. They won't go as high as in the Rockies, but they can go a bit higher than local trees all the same.

Thus we have the paradox in New Zealand of 'tropical' rainforest existing cheek by jowl with 'tundra' and even glaciers; two of which descend almost to sea level, or used to, before they started to get hammered by global warming in recent decades.

Since the rise of tramping in the 1920s, we have come more generally to realise that the New Zealand landscape and bush are in many ways unique and precious. But in pioneering days the bush really was viewed most often as a 'jungle' in the negative sense of the word, its tall trees valued mainly for what they would fetch at the timber-mill after they had been hacked down and civilisation advanced thereby. The pioneers would look on the bush with a shudder and, instead, go out of their way to make their towns and the farming districts around them look as much like England or Scotland as they could.

Gothic buildings would be erected amid beds of daffodils and other familiar flowers that would bloom in spring. And deciduous trees that would turn red and gold in autumn, and allow the winter sun and snow (if any) through their bare branches, would also be planted in preference to anything native.

Thus the French visitor André Siegfried said of a visit to Christchurch in 1904 that it had already the "strange, tranquil and respectable appearance of an old European city;" the townscape made English in every way in the course of less than sixty years of settlement.

This *faux*-Europeanness is most noticeable in the South Island. Towns in the North Island tend to be a bit more rough and ready, more obviously colonial and wooden in nature, with less use of brick and stone, and fewer deciduous trees as well.

A preference for building in wood rather than brick or stone, and a generally reduced effort in creating anything really permanent or an entirely new landscape, is partly due to the fact that most of the North Island was felt by the colonists to be more prone to earthquakes. As it turns out earthquakes are not unknown in the South, either: something we have lately been reminded of by the Christchurch earthquakes.

But as a result of attempts to create yet another New England, Arrowtown became famous for its autumn colours. Each region of New Zealand has its attractions, some of them primeval and native to the land, and others added in more recent times.

In 2010 there was a recession in New Zealand tourism. We lost the European and American markets for a while. Since the recovery buses have gone directly from Arrowtown to nearby Coronet and the Remarkables Ski Fields.

Being a single girl, my life quickly became unbearable. I went to Queenstown for entertainment, hiring hotel rooms for a couple of nights so I could see bands play.

Life during the day in Arrowtown was great, but at night it was quiet. Arrowtown has wonderful short walks. I loved tramping in the snow. My flatmate even did it at night when there was a full moon! He was from the United Arab Emirates and had been to a falcon training school there. He had moved to New Zealand and was now training falcons on Otago vineyards so that they would scare other birds away from the grapes.

We built a snowman together and adorned it with an 'agal', a black cord that encircles the head, worn by many Arab men. A most unusual accessory for a snowman. We ate hot marshmallows together in the backyard when the region was snowed in.

During one snow-in people took out their boogie boards and slid on the snow, carrying beers in their boots and letting their stereos blare, free to run amok as the place was closed off to the outside world.

Most days were sunny on the ski fields and, happily, there was no rain whatsoever, rain being something I had become allergic to in Auckland. After a few weeks down south, I went back to Auckland for a month. In Auckland it just rained, rained, and rained some more. Oh how I detested the rain!

Luckily I was back down South for the last two weeks of the ski season, and what a great season it was. The people out in the snow at night made it alive and pumping. I became acquainted with places like The Flame Restaurant, the Arrowtown Old Post Office, the New Orleans Hotel, the Botswana Butchery, The Halo, Atlas, and Póg Mahones. All had decent meals for under $20 on some nights of the week. I also discovered Arrowtown's best kept secret, an Indian Restaurant called the Mantra. I rounded it all off with Friday night skiing on Coronet Peak. It was blissful.

Winter in Arrowtown. Note the deciduous trees,
definitely not native to New Zealand.

The Arrowtown nightlife has definitely improved now. On a Monday night skiers can relax at the Blue Door, by the fire, with a wine from the cellar bar. There is a great movie theatre there called Dorothy Brown, with beanbags. Wanaka has the Ruby's.

Queenstown is full of online entrepreneurs, all selling their products on the internet. The region suits these people due to its cheap labour and low warehouse costs and, of course, because it's such a special place to live if you can work remotely. The town is even mentioned in bestselling book "*The 4-Hour Work Week*" by Timothy Ferriss, which encourages people to live wherever they want while escaping the drudgery of a nine to five work-week.

Some weekdays I was the only person with a Kiwi accent on the Remarkables ski field. There are special work permits granted to Argentinians, Brazilians and other internationals allowing them to work here for two years. (There are similar resorts in the Andes, notably San Carlos de Bariloche, a town that greatly resembles Queenstown and vice versa). All of this makes the Queenstown area a rich cultural hotspot.

WELCOME FLAT

After my stint in Arrowtown I finally went and worked as a warden at Welcome Flat. It had been in the back of my mind since it was suggested

Making a snowman

to me by that Auckland Tramping Club member.

En route I met and stayed with a local farming family in Whataroa, a small township an hour's drive from the township of Fox Glacier. I was warned by the farmer to watch out for the contract workers in the Fox Glacier Department of Conservation office. They said that the rangers were OK, apparently, but that the contractors were a bit backwards in their views.

The farmer showed me around his farm and bemoaned the lack of bees and frogs, which had steadily died off since he bought the farm thirty years ago.

He blamed the problem on artificial fertilisers and sprays, claiming that "When I bought this place it was swarming with bees and frogs, I used the ... company to fertilise the pasture and now there are no frogs or bees, they're all dead!" He had then formed his own fertilizer company, which used organic methods of drenching his cows, as he had real environmental concerns about what was happening to the bees and the frogs.

I had to prepare for taking ten days of food, plus my bedding, into the Welcome Flat Hut. My pack was really heavy, weighing in at twenty-seven kilograms. On my arrival at the Fox Glacier Department of Conservation base, I was greeted by a woman who was leaving the office *before* she was made redundant—a recurring theme I noticed at the Department of Conservation.

Another woman gave me an invoice book, a cash float, radio and radio battery, and tried to get me to take more stationery. I had to state rather emphatically that I couldn't add any more weight to my pack. I was also asked if I wanted to unload the coal bags that were being delivered by a helicopter over the next few days. These were dropped in via a four-metre high chute that held the coal storage for the hut. I politely refused, then sat down for some short lessons on how to operate the radio and understand what my responsibilities were as hut warden.

Following the steep Welcome Flat track littered with wet rocks (and carrying a heavy pack) was no easy feat. My pack was so weighed-down that I almost lost my balance on some of the flimsy wire bridges. However, I had seen far worse structures on the Harper Pass; more evidence of Department of Conservation fraying at the seams, even before the latest round of cutbacks. Some bridges seemed to have support bolts missing!

That sort of thing is an accident waiting to happen. A Department of Conservation footbridge I have crossed several times near Lake Waikaremoana in the North Island collapsed recently, tipping some trampers eight metres into the river below. Nobody was hurt: but that was quite literally a case of good luck and not good management. Ethical obligations aside it's ridiculous how the politicians keep under-funding the Department of Conservation when you think how important tourism is to the economy, not to mention the '100% Pure' and 'clean green' national image.

Leaving at nine a.m., I made it to the hut by six p.m. It was very hard going and my body was weary, but the scenery made up for it. The Sierra ranges and their coating of fast-melting snow provided a marvellous backdrop. One disappointing realisation was the lack of birdlife in the forest; the bush was very silent as I walked.

In 1837 an Australian species of possum had been liberated in New Zealand in the hope of establishing a fur trade. The American opossum is rat-like, but these Australian possums look like unusually large and furry domestic cats. Omnivorous, which is to say that they eat everything, the Australian possums promptly proceeded to devastate the New Zealand bush; which up to that time had not been browsed by any mammals apart from a small rat brought over by the Māori. Thirty years ago the possums had not yet reached the area around Welcome Flat in any numbers. But now the possums were everywhere. And the birds weren't.

Again, as with bridges and other infrastructure, the amount of effort that the Department of Conservation can put into keeping on top of pests such as the possums boils down entirely to the question of how much money and personnel they have to do the job.

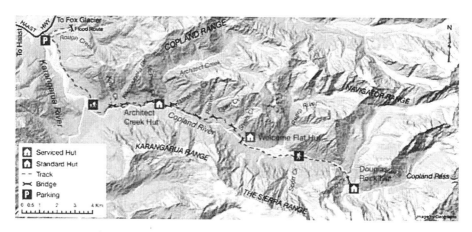

The Route to Welcome Flat from the Haast Highway
(from DOC brochure Copland Track to Welcome Flat Hut, 2012)

I made contact with Fox Base early the next morning and was told the helicopter was coming in with a load of coal and another ranger. They asked if I would mind him staying and I thought having company as protection would be good; the previous day I'd let two old men into the hut to sit out the rain and they'd stolen food from me!

The next night I was less tired and, lying awake, I could hear the avalanches falling from the peaks around me. The noise they make is like someone taking ice out of a bin at a party, but without the accompanying fun sounds of a party. I'd read about huts that had been totally wiped out along the track I had just walked. The last Welcome Flat hut had been bowled over by an avalanche with the ranger jumping out of the door to save his skin, a sandwich still in his mouth!

There are three hot pools at Welcome Flat — all with different temperatures — and they're divine. They were designed, constructed and built by Department of Conservation ranger Sally Jackson, who wrote a book called *Hot Springs of New Zealand*, published in 2006. Her book was written in the hut and details the locations of all of the hot pools in New Zealand.

I spotted a dead whio or blue duck on the riverbank, with its feathers strewn everywhere. It had been killed by possums or by some other kind of introduced pest; there's actually a long list of animals and plants brought in from overseas that have subsequently run amok in New Zealand.

There is no trapping in the valley and the locals are opposed to the use of 1080 pest-control poison (sodium fluoroacetate), even via hand application. This is another tough issue the Department faces, with compelling arguments on both sides. I did see one lonely whio on a rock; no doubt it was a surviving mate looking despondently for its lover.

The new ranger had previously worked for the United States Park Service. He'd relocated to Nelson, sold chai tea at the market and lived in a van on someone's land. He had some great stories to tell even though he was only twenty-five. A Buddhist, he used to meditate his Om anthem nude in the pools. He seemed an old soul to me, like a hippie out of the seventies, except he was young and fit and without the grey hair. It was like the days of the 1970s rock festivals all over again, festivals such as Sweetwaters and Nambassa in New Zealand back then. He struck me as just what we are missing in New Zealand today.

The ranger arrived in the helicopter, along with the local contractors whom the farmer had told me to avoid. One toothless character suggested we drink some beers but I declined and just got on with the job of helping them unload coal bags from the helicopter's net into the wheelbarrow.

Visitors to the hut included Buddhists from Byron Bay, a family of five, and a party of ten Asian migrant workers all on working visas from mainland China, Taiwan and Malaysia. Some of them had been employed at Treble Cone ski field, and others had been picking glasshouse tomatoes in Blenheim. None of them knew anything about Welcome Flat but they had decided to visit after being told to go there by a bus driver.

I was amazed at the stories the glasshouse tomato pickers told me. They said they got Repetitive Strain Injury (RSI) after a week doing the work and were paid only minimum wage, which was too low for them. Their experience was completely outside mine: an education for me.

After working as a warden at Welcome Flat I tramped up to Douglas Rock Hut, a day's walk further along the track. It was pouring with rain and when I arrived at the hut there was only green wood that wouldn't burn. Lacking the skills to make a fire out of new wood like a true scout, I put all my layers on and stayed in my sleeping bag to remain warm. I drank soup, tea and any hot substance I could find to keep me from getting cold.

The next stop after Douglas Rock Hut was just a shelter or bivvy, short for bivouac, called Copland Shelter. Shelters, or bivvys, have a roof but no walls. Some people prefer them because they are well-ventilated and close to nature, which is certainly true.

While I was at Copland Shelter I made friends with a family of eight kea, the world's only alpine parrot. They are known for their cheeky personalities and quite often break into cars and unattended backpacks to steal food and other items. Though they seem common because they are so readily attracted to carparks, campsites and unattended backpacks, kea are actually a threatened species. There are only about five thousand of them left and they are currently in decline, for the usual reasons.

Kea are intelligent and enjoy playing simple games. I gathered up ten small stones and placed them on a large rock. Then I would move one and a kea would move it back. I played this game with the kea family for over three hours! It was great to see the birds in their natural environment living off fern roots and other alpine shrubs. Amazingly, they left my pack alone because they were occupied with the rocks. Seeing them, let alone playing with them, was something I'll never forget. Sadly, this shelter is facing the threat of closure like many others. The week I spent on the West Coast went by so fast. Too fast!

After trekking out, I went to stay in Albert Town in Wanaka. I stayed with a flatmate after securing a room via the Easyroommate website. He was a mountain guide and the local radio station DJ.

I fell in love with the place and considered buying the former crib, or cabin, of Sir Edmund Hillary in Albert Town. The home had been extensively refurbished and bore little resemblance to the place Sir Ed stayed in but I still considered buying it.

Before making the decision I decided I would try out Albert Town as a renter first to see if I liked it. I discovered there was an Upper Clutha Tramping Club and used my flatmate's bike to explore everywhere; Upper Clutha, Lake Wanaka, into town — you name it, I biked there.

September is the down season for Wanaka, and the shoulder season for Queenstown. I met many qualified people like nurses and teachers who hadn't yet gained New Zealand qualifications or experience so they were working in places like supermarkets and gas stations.

Upper Clutha Tramping Club did a tramp to the Mount Aspiring Hut, up over the bush line and with views from almost the top of the Cascade range, overseeing the Matukituki River and Mount Aspiring, also known as Tititea or 'glistening peak', though in its case the English name is more familiar. Mount Aspiring National Park is magic. Crystal-clear rivers, glaciers, silver beech forests: it's a hiker's paradise.

The leader of the tramp was a 78 year-old dairy farmer, accompanied by his wife and two others. They were all far fitter than me and I followed them to the hut, constantly amazed by the vigour of these older people.

The local rest home ran Tai Chi classes. The old ladies there thought I was a reporter because I was asking questions and taking photos. One woman did Tai Chi with a parrot on her shoulder that wore a green nappy! I had never learnt so much about Tai Chi in such a short time. So, even though they were suspicious of my intent I'm glad they answered my questions.

In Albert Town I went to the movies and ate meals out with newly-made friends. But after a fortnight there I had nothing left to do. I thought that maybe Queenstown would be more my style. There was constant entertainment and I wouldn't see the same people three or four times a day.

In Queenstown I stayed at the backpacker's hostel run by a man called Rod. We became great friends and would eat our meals together, but I learnt pretty quickly to avoid mentioning the Treaty of Waitangi when talking to him. Rod did not believe in the Treaty at all. For him it was non-existent. He also believed the South Island was the mainland and ideally wanted it to be cut off from the North Island.

So much for Tino Rangatiratanga: the political cause of Māori sovereignty, upheld by many activists who argue that the Treaty of Waitangi should be restored to something like its original constitutional primacy. I don't think there was much market for that idea down in Queenstown. Just pronouncing Māori correctly in this part of New Zealand can elicit a negative reaction!

Ironically, this kind of racism is not caused by actual friction with Māori, but actually by the lack of it! For in the far south of New Zealand there are hardly any Māori at all. As such, the local Pākehā or whites are free to live on a diet of rumours about the Māori they hardly know.

A kind of laziness in New Zealand media coverage of Māori issues — a relentless diet of sensational stories about street crime in poverty-stricken and demoralised Māori neighbourhoods, angry-looking protestors and the occasional scuffle between the same and police, all presented in the spirit of 'if it bleeds, it leads' without history or context — doesn't help the South Islanders to form balanced opinions, either.

Basically, if all you watched was mainstream New Zealand TV and didn't actually know any Māori personally, you would get much the same idea about Māori in places like Auckland that you would get about the Black Lives Matter movement in the USA, if all you watched were Fox News and the Crime and Investigation channel.

These biases are endlessly picked over by academics; but unfortunately few people in New Zealand pay attention to what academics have to say.

After my few weeks in the scenic but also rather provincial South Island I headed back to Auckland: which unfortunately also now seemed liked being in a prison cell to me, but for different reasons. After seeing the majesty of the South Island, the Waitakere Ranges didn't do it for me anymore.

TIRITIRI MATANGI

I saw the fireworks launching the 2011 Rugby World Cup in Auckland from the Tiritiri Matangi Island lighthouse.

I'd landed there a few days earlier to volunteer as a ranger, working with the Co-ordinator of Volunteers who knew where every single kiwi and tuatara was on the island.

Kiwi were so common there you could just about fall over them during the day. I met one bird, a takahē, known as 'Lonely Greg', an old patriarch who'd lost a battle with one of the other dominant males and now spent most of his time by himself. Lonely Greg was fed on plant supplements and had a monitor so that he wouldn't die alone. He has since passed.

Tai Chi with a parrot

There was a profusion of birdlife on the island. Takahē, a flightless blue fowl related to the smaller pukeko (which can still fly), were a species whose peeping cries to one another sounded prehistoric to me. There were also kōkako, a songbird whose calls were very different, deep and mysterious — sounding even more primordial.

There was a group of zoologists on the island, all studying the birdlife. One was completing research for a PhD on the tiny wren-like species known most commonly as the rifleman, its Māori name titipounamu. Like the cabbage tree, the rifleman is another exception to the rule that most New Zealand animals and plants have retained their Māori names in common usage. The other zoologists were catching kōkako and kākāriki, a small green parrot, in nets and taking excrement samples in order to determine if any diseases had become prominent in the island's bird populations.

Tiritiri Matangi had been planted with native trees in 1995 and even though it's only two decades on, they're well-established and look like they've been there for much longer. There is also a gift shop on the island staffed by volunteers from Auckland, one of whom told me that during World War II the military had blasted the island's last refuge for New Zealand long-tailed bats, which resulted in the local extinction of the species. She was fiercely protective of Tiritiri Matangi and said that only over her dead body would any government department take over the management of this island!

I was now addicted to volunteering. On my return to Auckland City I applied for volunteer work on Stewart Island which is officially known by the bilingual name of Stewart Island/Rakiura, and on Whenua Hou ('new land'), a still smaller island known in settler terminology as Codfish Island.

THE ISLAND OF BLUSHING SKIES

The meanings of Māori place names are sometimes clear and obvious, but also sometimes contested even among Māori, as old-time Māori were much given to poetical allusions.

Nineteenth-century missionary societies, to their credit, contended as proof of universal equality that supposedly primitive peoples often had complicated languages that took European missionaries years to learn, and traditions of oratory and poetry that were quite sophisticated as well. And so it was with Māori, though the basics of the language are not too hard to pick up. Māori place names are often abbreviations of longer sayings which carry layers of obscure poetical meaning.

Whenua Hou or 'New Land' seems obvious enough, as unmistakable as the settlers' plain-as-a-pikestaff Codfish Island. On the other hand Rakiura is more allusive. It is thought to be short for Te Rakiura a Te Rakitamau, 'the great blush of Te Rakitamau', a reference in an old, now-extinct southern Māori dialect to a young man refused the hand of two successive women in marriage.

At the same time it is thought that Rakiura, the great blush, is not the ultimate meaning, and that it is really a poetical allusion to the glowing skies of the aurora australis, the southern counterpart of the more familiar aurora borealis; or, just as conceivably, to long summer twilights or gloamings. Rangi in northern, living, official Māori means sky; its old southern cognate is raki. And ura is a word that means a reddish glow. So, Rakiura seems to mean the Island of Blushing Skies, a much more poetical name than Stewart Island.

For we are indeed getting pretty far south here, into essentially Patagonian latitudes in which, to borrow an image from the New Zealand poet Sam Hunt, curtains of fire do swish about under the stars of dead cold south just as they do in the frozen north; the Ísland and the not-so-Greenland.[1]

The effect is aided by the fact that the South Magnetic Pole around with the auroras cluster is actually closer to New Zealand than one might think. The North Magnetic Pole is near the geographical North Pole but the South Magnetic Pole is at present outside the Antarctic Circle and south-west of New Zealand (the two magnetic poles are not exactly in line). In the year

1   Sam Hunt, 'Of the star of the dead cold south', in *Collected Poems, 1963-1980*, Auckland, Penguin Books, 1980

1600 it is estimated that it lay at 80 degrees south latitude, almost due south of New Zealand.

So, you might not think Rakiura was still part of Polynesia if it were not for the poetical names — it's a long, long way from Hawai'i and Tahiti down here.

I was to be doing track maintenance and helping to look after the kākāpō, the famous flightless parrot, starting the following March.

I also had plans to tramp the challenging Dusky Sound Track in the middle of Fiordland in New Zealand's wild south-west (the Atawhenua, the Shadowland); as well as the Hump Ridge Track just outside of Tuatapere close to New Zealand's southernmost city, Invercargill — where the people are supposed to be the most welcoming to visitors among all New Zealanders, since it really is the end of the line down there.

THE BEST SUNSET IN NEW ZEALAND

The Hump Ridge Track is managed by a charitable trust through a partnership formed between the Department of Conservation and the community. The night before the tramp I stayed in a backpacker hostel. Unfortunately, as I was trying to get to sleep, the other hostel guests started partying and began doing wheelies outside my window.

At three a.m. I rang the owner of the backpackers and told him I couldn't sleep and added that I hoped he couldn't either! Eventually at four a.m. they quieted down. I was livid.

After a patchy night's sleep I started down the track and soon met a cigarette-smoking businessman from Hamilton who threw his lit cigarettes in the bush as he was tramping! "Excuse me," I exclaimed, "don't you have a mobile ashtray or somewhere else you can put them?!" He shook his head and said, "Oh okay, sure." But he didn't stop, his disrespect was infuriating!

I also met and tramped with a Dutch girl who'd been trekking around New Zealand for four months. The sunset on the first night was incredible: a sky rainbow of oranges and reds, and you could even see Stewart Island in the distance. The Island of Blushing Skies, indeed!

After completing the Hump Ridge track I returned to the same hostel in Tuatapere, where the owner kindly refunded my first night's fees, gave me a free night and a lift to Invercargill the next day. That famous southern hospitality more than made up for my issues on the first night.

Once in Invercargill I met the Department of Conservation manager responsible for volunteer hut wardens, who took me shopping in Invercargill to get me the food I needed for a two-week stint at the Port William Hut on Stewart Island, the start of the Rakiura Track. For actually places like Tuatapere and Invercargill — honoured since 1908 in the Invercargill March, a popular if somewhat traditional brass band favourite — aren't quite the end of the line. There's still a bit further to go; but now you have to get your feet wet.

STEWART ISLAND AS IT IS

In the largest settlement on Stewart Island, Oban, I met Phil Brooks, the Department of Conservation Manager in charge of volunteers. Phil has since relocated to Motueka. He took me through the safety checks, taught me how to operate the radio and detailed what was expected of me while at the hut.

The Rakiura Track is officially classed in New Zealand as a Great Walk, meaning a premier tramping route mainly aimed at tourists, but it doesn't provide gas cooking facilities at its huts. I was to hear that roughly half of the staff on Stewart Island were being made redundant due to local review. There was also talk of closing the North West circuit on the island, which is a free camping spot for a lot of people. Many Department of Conservation staff have invested in local communities like Stewart Island and some also have young children who are part of these communities. I believe that there needs to be some government responsibility for supporting these people, a social contract of some kind.

Actually this is a pervasive problem of public service in an isolated

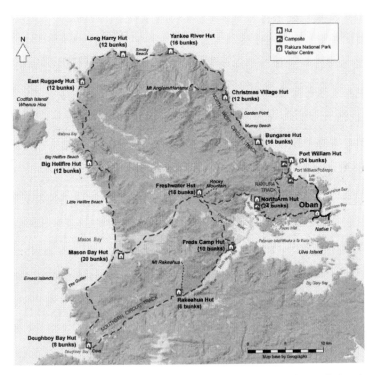

The northern part of Stewart Island/Rakiura, with Cod sh Island / Whenua Hou at top left (from DOC Brochure North West and Southern Circuit Tracks, Rakiura National Park, May 2015)

country like New Zealand, where the labour market is small, and often vanishingly small where unusual skills are concerned.

People who work in government often have a vocation, quite literally, for public service. They often invest years of their time in unusual skills understood by few others, skills that have no real private sector application, only to get the flick in some restructuring driven by a calculation in a spreadsheet. I really don't think the average politician gets this issue at all. They imagine, 'Oh well, our laid-off biologist specialising in rare bats, or urban public transport planner, or expert at dealing with young kids getting into trouble in gangs, can always become a manager at an import warehouse'.

Well, er, no. Life's not quite as simple as that. And it does undermine commitment and vocation to have constant redundancies and shakeups.

Would the politicians rather have public servants who were highly committed and expert even if they *were* sometimes a bit weird and bearded, or a bit over-cautious?

Or would the politicians rather have serried ranks of 'hollow suits' who knew that their jobs were insecure from day one, that they would be judged on how much money they could save and how quickly, and who knew that they probably won't be around long enough to be face the consequences of slashing the regulatory or maintenance budget because by that stage they'll either have been made redundant or accepted a better offer in the private sector? Maybe, even, from the firms that aren't being regulated so closely any more?

I would argue that the first is obviously the more robust long-term option for public management. But it's very old-fashioned by the standards of how things are done in New Zealand at present.

Port William on Stewart Island, where I worked as a hut warden, has a

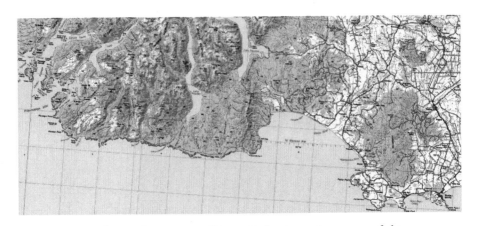

*Hump Ridge and Environs. Hump Ridge is at the centre of this map,
running north-south at the western end of the large curving bay known
as Te Waewae Bay. This coastline looks south toward Stewart Island.
Fiordland is at left, and agricultural Southland to the right.*
(Land Information New Zealand, *via NZTopomaps*)

very early European history. Its name seems to be a nod to Fort William, a town in the northern highlands of Scotland; the sort of name that is par for the course in Scottish-settled Otago and Southland.

An early attempt was made at logging at Port William, but substantial settlement was impossible due to its extreme isolation. It was hard to get food shipped to the Port William harbour and people often went hungry. The infrequency of shipping also made it hard to get the logs out of the port in order to pay for supplies. Thus began a downward spiral of flagging industry and dwindling food.

Port William was forsaken by an empire that soon retreated to more convenient harbours such as Invercargill and Dunedin.

And it is in that sense that Invercargill, a reasonably impressive city, is the end of the line after all. At Invercargill we are in a southernmost province of

New Zealand that is comparable to Iceland, isolated but still citified. Beyond that point things become more existential: a land of small settlements and vast silences of sea and sky.

I met many people from the Auckland Tramping Club and the Auckland Catholic Tramping Club while on Stewart Island, and it was with the Catholic Club that I was to see sooty shearwaters or tītī in Māori, also known as mutton birds, landing at night and going into their burrows. It was a magical moment. There are estimated to be over twenty million of these birds around New Zealand, mostly near Stewart Island, and three hundred thousand are harvested by the southern Māori iwi or tribe of Ngai Tahu every year, a number that is fully sustainable. A delicacy in the lower South Island, you can even purchase mutton bird meat in ordinary butchers' shops in Dunedin.

The settlers called it mutton bird because the flesh is dark and fatty and looks like mutton when cooked. But actually it tastes like anchovies, with a strong, salty, oily and smelly fish flavour. We are talking about a kind of seagull, of course: and you can imagine what a seagull must taste like. Like olives, red-hot curries and strongly-flavoured cheese, mutton bird or tītī is an acquired taste. If it is to be eaten in large amounts, it should be boiled in water that is repeatedly thrown away and replaced to remove the salt and excessive fishiness. Otherwise, it is more like a garnish. Actually, these days it is too costly to eat in large amounts: but back in the day it was quite possibly all people had. Oysters, too, were once the food of the poor...

As a warden at Port William I had to clean toilets and sweep the hut. I also had to put out fires at the camp site, a two hour walk away, and collect hut tickets. It wasn't demanding work — the main thing was that somebody had to be there to do it.

Deer hunters staying at the Port William camp site tended to hang their dead deer from trees, which shocked many of the younger trampers. Most of the hunters asked the trampers if they wanted to try some of the venison, and when they did they were very impressed with the rich smoky flavours.

I was at Port William in the 'Roaring Season', which begins in mid-March, when the stags fight one another over the fertile females. As well as deer, feral cats were numerous on the Stewart Island and the local Department of Conservation office was, once again, doing very little to control numbers.

The Stewart Island kiwi is known locally as Porky because it's stockier than its North Island cousins. It also comes out during the day. The first night I was at the hut I spotted one with my red-LED torch and on the last night I ended up with a kiwi sitting on my boot for a full two minutes! As warden I would instruct guests to only use a red-LED torch when attempting to view the kiwi by night.

Like most animals that prowl about at night, kiwi are insensitive to red light. When the eye of any creature, including a human being, is adapted to darkness, it loses the ability to perceive the colour red and shifts its sensitivity toward the blue end of the spectrum. Thus red objects appear black by moonlight but blue objects appear white.

Have you ever noticed that? It is uncanny once pointed out. People sometimes think that the effect comes about because moonlight is blue. But in fact the 'blueness' of moonlight is an illusion. Moonlight is just the same colour as daylight. This is a fact easily demonstrated by taking a long-exposure colour photograph under moonlight, which produces a scene resembling daytime. The truth is that our eyes alter their perception under moonlight in such a way that red literally drops out of the picture.

Exposed to bright light, our eye reverts to 'normal' daytime perception. But for many nocturnal creatures, from domestic cats to kiwi, the eye is perpetually dark-adapted.

What that means is that not only is the animal somewhat colour-blind by our standards, but also that even quite a bright red light is a nearly or completely invisible 'black light' as far as it is concerned. Thus a red light is effectively the same as infrared night vision for the purpose of seeing nocturnal creatures going about their nightly business; with the advantage that we don't need special goggles to see them, while they can't see us.

A further advantage is that red light will not greatly affect our own dark-adapted eye. If the light is suddenly switched off we will still be able to see the 'blue' world of the night, whereas a white light would have blinded us. Thus on all counts a red light, above all the pure red light of a red LED, is perfect for spotting creatures such as kiwi at night.

I discovered the possums were eating the campers' food at the Port William campsite so I took the initiative to lay three traps — and straight away killed three possums. Other conservancies have vegetarian wardens who refuse to kill possums. Though taking a life is never easy, the possums are pests known for killing the chicks of kea and kaka as well as damaging the native bush.

The aforementioned 1080 is a controversial substance: it's not used at all in some areas, such as the Wilkin and Young Valleys in Mount Aspiring National Park. The Department of Conservation (called DOC for short, incidentally) hand-lays 1080 poison in some other areas rather than doing helicopter drops. This satisfies the deer hunters as a heli-drop kills deer as well as its intended targets.

In fact much of the opposition to 1080, a poison which usually kills mammals while sparing birds, and is thus perfect for reverting the New Zealand wilderness to its original pre-human ecology, comes from deer hunters: which is ironic because deer are also considered to be an introduced pest, strictly speaking.

In an ideal world DOC would be quite happy to wipe out the deer in addition to other mammalian pests: to organise an ultimate heli-drop of 1080 from one end of the country to the other, *Apocalypse Now*-style.

Thus, a solution to our ecological problems is quite simple in principle. Yet DOC is up against a significant hunter lobby which insists that the Conservation Department drive with the handbrake on in its conservation efforts, so that the deer are spared. And it's also fair to say that even people sympathetic to the conservation cause are a unhappy about the idea of exterminating millions of cute furry animals with sharp teeth, now that there are in fact millions of them to exterminate. Such are the 'triangulations' which conservation authorities must pursue in the real world of politics in New Zealand, and elsewhere.

When it came to the end of my stay on Stewart Island, I discovered that the next volunteer had cancelled — so they asked me to stay on for another two weeks.

The average temperature of Stewart Island during its warmest month is normally less than fourteen degrees Celsius. Even so, during the warm months of February and March when I was there, Stewart Island was a Pacific Island paradise: hot and sunny and ringing with birdsong. When I walked to other huts I could hear the sound of the fishermen's radios mingling with the calls of the birds. It was absolute bliss and I was more than happy to stay for an extra fortnight.

KĀKĀPŌ ON CODFISH ISLAND / WHENUA HOU

After a month on Stewart Island I was off to Whenua Hou or Codfish Island. Whenua Hou is a reserve dedicated to the recovery of the native flightless parrot, the Kākāpō, and is located three kilometres northwest of Stewart Island.

Before departing for the island I didn't know if I was flying in an airplane or taking a helicopter ride. I was petrified because in the 1990s I had taken a tourist helicopter ride over the Shotover River near Queenstown and felt like I was falling out of the sky. To my relief, our transport was a four-seater plane from Invercargill Airport.

Unfortunately, the weather was wet and windy and the pilot was very quiet and even sweating as he attempted to land. It took two attempts before we managed to land.

When we landed I had to go through a very strict and thorough security check. To be allowed onto the island you have to go through quarantine. During the process they checked for foreign grasses in my socks and other gear, so I had made sure to purchase new socks as well as washing my pack and all of my wet weather gear before I did go.

The kākāpō is an owl-like flightless parrot that is dangerously close to extinction. There are only roughly one hundred and thirty left in the world. Ferrets and possums almost wiped the species out and, sadly, conservation authorities left it too late before intervening, an oversight which has led to a small gene pool.

The use of modern science has helped to expand the gene pool and conservationists are using artificial insemination to increase numbers. So, Whenua Hou is a pretty special place: one of the few places on earth you can see kākāpō. They're susceptible to viruses due to their lack of genetic diversity. While I was there a sick kākāpō had to be taken to hospital in Invercargill, where he later died.

Track maintenance on Whenua Hou was hellish. We were set to work ripping up seventy metres of track with crowbars and staple-gunning down new track in its place, all this done in the rain of course! My back just about gave out after five days of this.

The breeding season on Whenua Hou is a busy affair. Rangers use the wooden walkways on the island 24/7 for about two months, travelling to and from the nests and monitoring the kākāpō. Once the birds are nesting, volunteers camp outside the burrows and monitor the comings and goings of the parents. There are cameras placed in every nest to monitor the incubation period. When the eggs hatch each chick is more precious than gold. They're weighed, hand-fed, and all the growth processes overseen. The success of a breeding season depends on the abundance of berries from a tree called rimu, and there are numerous berry collection points throughout the island. Though much effort is made to keep the kākāpō fed, the rangers tend to lose a lot of weight while on the job, as there's so much ground to cover.

The start of the breeding cycle begins with the male kākāpō's booming song, a mating call designed to attract the females. Some males are far more successful than others at this. But for the less adept males, artificial insemination is also being used to diversify the gene pool. This process is essential because some breeding-age males, like Richard Henry's son Sirocco, were hand-reared and now prefer the company of humans to other birds.

I met some of the kākāpō juveniles during the day that were being weighed. Hand-rearing does occur but it is preferable the chicks are raised in the wild as it can affect their breeding potential later on. Poor Sirocco may never mate with another kākāpō but he has other pleasures. In an oft-replayed scene from a British nature documentary, he is famous for making out with the BBC cameraman and zoologist Mark Carwardine's head.

The conservationists are aiming to increase the population of kākāpō across the three offshore New Zealand islands, Whenua Hou, Anchor Island and Little Barrier Island. It's amazing to think that kākāpō once actually lived up and down Aotearoa.

How could anyone stand by and see a species almost wiped out? It is unfathomable to me. A man named Richard Henry, the namesake of an aforementioned kākāpō, attempted to transfer a number of the birds to Resolution Island in Fiordland where he was working as caretaker in the 1890s. Unfortunately, around 1900, stoats arrived on the island and decimated the populations he had established.

I did a lot of hiking after working so hard and took photographs of yellow-eyed penguins. The DOC rangers also asked me to do track foundation work but I said I was not a carpenter. They were pleased with the rest of my work and that was the main thing.

When it came time to leave we had to take the helicopter out instead of the four-seater plane because of the high winds. I silently freaked out but let no one know how I was feeling. I was given instructions in helicopter etiquette: keep your head down when landing, clear the landing area for loose debris, never approach the back of the helicopter because of the blades and so on. We loaded it up and when we took off I was very relieved! I had imagined something else based on my last experience but to my surprise it was a far calmer ride than the four-seater plane. I loved the ride over Stewart Island and we made a very smooth landing in Invercargill.

HELP!

My stint at volunteering was exciting but I felt like tramping. I headed to the remote Dusky Sound Track; a challenging rough muddy track with regular flooding. I knew it would be tough, but I didn't realise exactly how tough it would be.

To prepare for the tramp I packed ten days' worth of food — salami and cheese every day for lunch, porridge for breakfast and Backcountry Cuisine (a range of meals that are geared for adventurers) for dinner. I'm not a fan of salami because I loathe processed meat but you can't be fussy when you have limited space for food in your pack. By the time I was packed, my gear weighed in at 25kg (and that was without a 3kg tent).

I got the boat across Lake Hauroko, a deep alpine lake, to the first hut. The weather was great for this part of the journey (there was a drought in place) but the 'bridges' were unstable.

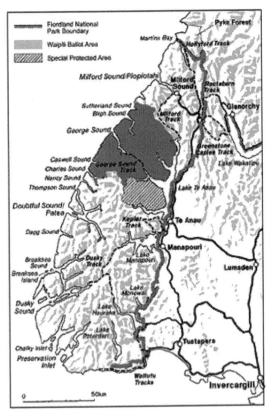

Great Walks in Fiordland (DOC)

They were just wire crossings, where you stand on a wire and hold onto another one, and I just about fell off every single one due to the weight of my pack. I ended up doing river crossings instead of using the 'bridges' and followed deer trails into the bush and to the river's edge.

I felt like a real explorer (but would have preferred that the track had been better maintained). The scenery was mind- blowing; U-shaped valleys, tree-covered mountainous peaks, wild deer, flourishing birdlife and glacial lakes. I later was told they maintain the track every two years, not that you would have known.

I now realise I should never have attempted Dusky Sound alone, although I do concentrate more when I tramp by myself. While on the tramp I lost my water bottle and fell over numerous trees. The huts were full of rats and mice (a phobia of mine) so I ended up sleeping outside on a hut mattress with thousands of sandflies. Not ideal but preferable to the rodent-guests inside the hut. To protect my pack I placed it on top of the long drop toilets. It felt a bit weird but it worked; my gear was untouched by vermin of any description.

My luck ran out when I fell waist-deep into some mud. I had to climb a tree to get out and my pack nearly sank into the bog. I pulled my calf muscle extricating myself and my pack from the mud. Once I was out I realised I could barely move so I let off the locator beacon. I wasn't worried; I knew that my signal was strong so it was just a matter of time until I was found, so I sat down and made a cup of tea. I had a fortnight's worth of food and the weather was clear so I embraced the wait.

The helicopter flew over. It was searching for me using GPS coordinates and I quickly realised I could not be seen where I was sitting. I dragged myself sideways on to a rock by the river. I waved and waved and waved with my walking stick until my arm hurt and eventually they spotted me.

A kākāpō. The name means 'night parrot' for, in addition to being flightless, they mostly come out at night. This is unusual for birds, and puts kākāpō in the same company as owls and kiwi.

The helicopter descended and I was hooked up to a harness and winched up above the tree line. I'm usually scared of heights but this time I wasn't because I just wanted to get out of there. I just relaxed into the ropes and enjoyed the view.

I had one heck of a helicopter ride to Te Anau over Lake Manapouri. It's like flying over a landscape best-of: prehistoric mountains with snow-capped tips, and all the waterways eating into the native bush-covered land. It was breath-taking.

After that experience I had to rest my calf muscle for three weeks, get acupuncture treatment and organise replacement EFTPOS and credit cards (I'd lost them somewhere on the track). Then I discovered that they'd been picked up by a member of the Auckland Tramping Club and handed to someone in Wanaka to pick up. Oh no, the Auckland Tramping Club had found out about my rescue! Blush.

The ambulance officer in the helicopter told me that many foreigners just call them when they are tired or for other weird reasons, and in those cases they're made to pay for their rescue. But I wasn't. I'd genuinely injured myself; it wasn't like I set off my beacon because I couldn't handle the tramp. As my rescuer said, it's better to be safe rather than sorry.

Unfortunately, when I failed to make the return boat out of Dusky Sound I was reported as a missing person for 24 hours. Search and Rescue didn't communicate with the police about my rescue and I didn't tell the boat operator I'd left Dusky Sound via helicopter. I was in a mixture of shock and exhaustion and forgot; but I assumed that the rescue services (who were on the radio) would communicate with the others. They didn't.

I was at the backpackers in Te Anau, without my EFTPOS or credit cards, when a policeman arrived and, in front of fifty people, said he wanted

Tongariro crossing

to talk to me. I let him know I was OK and in the end he apologised after it became clear that the rescue agencies had failed to communicate with each other about my rescue.

After three weeks of acupuncture my pulled calf muscle had healed and I was able to do the Rees-Dart Track. One of New Zealand's most beautiful tramps, the Dart Glacier retains its status as the most beautiful glacier I have ever been on, because from there you can see Mount Aspiring, which looks a bit like the Matterhorn in Switzerland, and the gorgeous valley towards Wanaka. Plus it's easier to access it so you're not exhausted by the time you get there.

Auckland Tramping Club bus

In May 2012, I bought a unit in Queenstown and now I commute between there and Auckland. I have fond memories of Auckland; but in Queenstown I can see the Main Divide from my bedroom window (and I never need to pull my curtains for privacy reasons).

I've learnt that I can be happy wherever I decide to be, and for me enjoying the Southern Alps is ultimately preferable to constantly travelling to Europe. In New Zealand, we have it all. Rather than cutting back Department of Conservation funding, we must learn to protect what we have.

Yet we have had a succession of insensitive governments, high suicide rates, child poverty, family violence and obesity in this supposed paradise. I have to ask myself, why?

If you are interested to know more about trekking in New Zealand, check out *A Maverick New Zealand Way*.

CHAPTER TWENTY-NINE
Peter the Great's Home Town

Iɴ September 2013 I decided to go to St Petersburg, the cultural centre of Russia. It was founded in 1703 by the former Tsar Peter the First, 'Peter the Great', one of the most powerful monarchs in the world at that time. He was given the nickname 'the great' after he introduced a cultural revolution and extensive visionary reforms to Russia: modernising education, administration, his country's defence, commerce, industry and technology.

I call St Petersburg the city of palaces — the turn of every corner seems to open a vista onto something ornate and lavish. With around thirty palaces there were more than I'd seen in my whole life in one place.

After so many years of travelling on a backpacker's budget I felt like a splurge so booked into a five-star hotel for a few nights. I was disappointed. It was clean, but that was all that was going for it. The décor was dated and tasteless. It was stuck in the nineties and it certainly wasn't worth the $300 per night I'd paid!

I always need Wi-Fi in accommodation so I can check in on my rental properties and rent books and communicate with my property managers if needed. I logged into the hostel's system through 'Putin's Network'—which I found amusing. It was less amusing as events transpired, more on that later though.

So, I get my work done and the next morning I'm questioned by the porter in reception.

"Goodness me you do a lot of work on the internet don't you?" He wanted to know what sort of work I did, why I had used so much data last night (according to him) and various other quite personal things. Putin's Network... hmmm...

I decided that being under a microscope and a dated room was not worth $300 so I looked for somewhere else to stay.

I showed up at the first place ready to check in. Actually, I was checked in by a uniformed official who ticked me off as "arriving," but then told me that hostel was fully booked so I needed to go to the other side of the city to the other part of the hostel, as the accommodation was split between two properties ten kilometres apart.

I remember feeling like I was under surveillance and my actions were being recorded. One woman followed me around. When I asked her why she was stalking me she said she wanted to practise her English because she

Pussy Riot. I met the drummer — the photographs and placards here were part of a display at an art museum.

was a student. I wasn't convinced.

At the time, quite a few of my Facebook friends were members of Greenpeace. The famous environmental organisation had been protesting in a very high-profile way about Russian oil drilling in the Arctic and two members from New Zealand had been put in prison in Russia. I remember a friend asking me to get them out! But I wasn't able to; I was there on my own and worried about being put in jail myself. It was a stressful and difficult situation.

I noticed more people following me around, wherever I went. Maybe this semi-accidental Greenpeace connection really did have something to do with it. I got a bit annoyed really, because I didn't travel all the way to St Petersburg to be followed around by anyone and everyone. I really just wanted to stay under the radar while I was here, thank you very much.

I decided I wasn't going to stay in the two-part hostel anymore, so I found a one-bedroom place with ten beds all in the one room. All the other guests were male: all from Albania.

I felt safer here staying in a room with 9 male strangers than I did in the other place! The Albanian men were super respectful, very tidy and worked long hours (so they weren't around much). The location was fantastic; close to everything I needed and wanted to be part of.

On the third day, I went into a copy centre to get the photos extracted from my camera and ended up meeting the drummer from the band Pussy Riot; which, if anyone was spying on me and it wasn't just my imagination, must have removed all doubt. For, Pussy Riot was a popular anti-Putin feminist band that was causing quite a scandal in Russia. They donned colourful balaclavas and protested about women's rights. There was one main incident in 2012 where the group performed in protest against the Russian Orthodox Church's support for Putin. The two main singers were jailed for their part which led to quite a bit of international media attention, especially when the likes of Björk, Paul McCartney and Lady Gaga made their support for the group's action's public. This boosted Pussy Riot's media attention and even lead to Amnesty International getting involved in the case. The atmosphere at the time in Russia wasn't really that great. A guy that was with them invited me to a Pussy Riot punk rock evening. It reminded me of the New Zealand music scene in the late 1970s when all kinds of radicals were being spied on back home.

I did consider their offer but then thought, no way! They seemed to get themselves into a bit of trouble, which I didn't really need. First Greenpeace, now Pussy Riot: there was no sense adding further pages to a dossier of what Russian officialdom might consider to be my doubtful connections.

* * *

The Winter Palace is a grand mint-green and white baroque building a quarter of a kilometre long, with 117 staircases and nearly two thousand windows. It was impressive and over-the-top as well. I walked around the outside of it because it was only open to the public on certain days, and it was closed the day I wanted to visit.

I wasn't confident enough to hire a car so I did tours, caught the bus and walked everywhere. St Petersburg by day is very different than by night. In the evening all the buildings are lit with decorative lights so the city twinkles.

Russia used to allow all night drinking where you could drink till seven in the morning. But they had changed it to be similar to New Zealand's drinking rules, where bars wouldn't allow any new people to enter after a certain time. In Russia if you were in that bar drinking past one o'clock, you had to stay there. If you left you weren't allowed back in. So, I felt quite safe wandering around at night (even though I felt like I was being watched by the government). One thing I could not get over while I was in St Petersburg was the quality of the food. Everything was fresh. I honestly believe that they have the best restaurants in the world. You could order anything at all and it tasted like everything had been picked straight out of the garden. I fell in love with the Russian beetroot salads, something I'd never been a fan of in New Zealand. For around $8 a day I ate amazing meals: succulent steak, beautiful soups, and everything was prepared straight in front of me. There was no microwave cooking here! Ordinary Russians could afford to eat well in St Petersburg. It contrasted with the images of people queuing for bland grey food that I'd seen in media reports over the years.

The Mariinsky Palace was another highlight. A majestic salmon-coloured building that was converted into a hospital during World War II started off as a wedding gift from Tsar Nicolas I to his daughter. It's an elaborate building filled with decorative columns, gold embellishments, oversized chandeliers and marble. And it was wheelchair-friendly: the Tsar's daughter had a medical condition so there are ramps throughout the palace. How's that for a present?!

The Mariinsky Theatre looked like a smaller version of the Winter Palace; it was in the same colour palette. After it opened in 1860, some of Russia's foremost composers debuted their works there including Tchaikovsky. And in later years it was the preferred performance space for opera stars and ballet greats like Rudolf Nureyev and Anna Pavlova. It was also the home for influential and renowned choreographer Marius Petipa who created such masterpieces like *The Nutcracker, Sleeping Beauty* and *Swan Lake*, which became the most famous ballet of them all. With such a rich history, I was excited to be there.

When I arrived, I found that I was in a stall with a twenty Russian Army

Officers. Because my seat was in the middle of a row I jumped over the seats with my shoes on. I nearly got arrested. One of the Army Officers shouted that I was behaving like a monkey and if I didn't watch out he'd have me arrested. I was embarrassed. I guess when you go backpacking around for so long you do get a bit sloppy.

I saw Swan Lake inside the theatre. Looking around the ornate cream, eggshell blue and gold interior took me back in time to the golden era of Russian ballet. It was amazing. I later saw the Bolshoi Ballet perform but I felt that this was better.

Walking around St Petersburg with a backpack was frowned upon. I noticed not a lot of people did that; I got many glares from locals and I guess when you're in St Petersburg you're supposed to dress accordingly. Everyone dresses up here. In hindsight, I should also have put my backpack in the storage place at reception, at the Mariinsky Theatre.

But my tour of theatres and palaces was far from over.

The Catherine Palace in Tsarskoye Selo, a suburb of St Petersburg, looks as though it's straight out of a Disney cartoon. Bright blue and gold and extravagantly detailed, it's the happiest-looking palace I've ever seen. It was the summer residence for the Tsars, because of course you can't use the same palace all year around, and 100 kilograms of gold were used to decorate the exterior when it was first built. Rumour has it that the roof was made entirely out of gold too! The ballroom was bananas. There was so much gold around the windows and artworks I could hardly see the paintwork underneath.

Tsarskoye Selo was occupied by the Germans during World War II, and the Catherine Palace was used as an army barracks. It was looted by the Nazi forces once they realised that they were going to have to retreat, and gutted by fire. What we see today is a faithful reconstruction based on the fact that the shell of the building survived, plus photographs, paintings and plans made before its wartime destruction. The epic reconstruction is still ongoing.

The Peterhof Palace, one of the homes of Peter the Great, is known as the Russian Versailles. The entry staircase to the palace is flanked with gold statues, fountains and majestic gardens. Built in 1703, the imposing yellow and white building was almost destroyed during World War II as well. But extensive restoration work after the war returned it to its original magnificence. I stood there looking over the water to the Gulf of Finland — thinking I'd love to go to Finland too one day.

While I was on these tours I met loads of people. One was a retired astrophysicist from the United States of America looking for a Russian wife.

We had plenty of interesting discussions about outer space and inhabiting Mars. He was fascinating. I often wonder if he found what he was looking for.

I also met three Americans looking for Russian women to bed. But they complained that the women dressed like princesses and were all ready to get married, rather than be seduced, so they were out of luck. I suggested they go and find some prostitutes!

The person that stood out the most was a twenty-three year old Singaporean woman who was hanging out with the Russian Mafia and taking far too many drugs. She showed me how to transfer money on the black market. But even though I thought about it (the rates were better) the 'money exchanges' were all in dark dingy places. So, I preferred the legit way. It made me sad; but people make their own choices even if they're risky and stupid.

Mostly though, I met locals.

There were a number of Albanian girls working in the kitchen at the hostel I was staying in. I remember them telling me that they were only paid about $60 a week. Even though that seemed a pittance, it was more than the wage that cleaners and receptionists got: around $180 per month!

I had intended to go to Belarus next before Moscow and I was pre-warned not to drink the water there because it was too close to where Chernobyl was, five hours south by road. This advice sounded a bit over-the-top, but it hinted at real concerns. Even though at that time twenty-seven years had passed, it was shocking that the catastrophic nuclear disaster was still affecting people. Although only thirty-one people died during the explosion and its immediate aftermath, it is estimated that around six thousand people died in subsequent years from radiation exposure related to the blast, including many who were involved in the clean-up. Up to five million people were affected in some way, whether through economic, physical health or psychological issues.

I had intended to take the train through to Belarus so got a taxi to the train station in St Petersburg. But it wasn't as smooth a ride as I expected. I said to the taxi driver that I needed to get to the train before mid-day today and his reaction was crazy. He started yelling and screaming, "Don't you dare tell me what to do!"

I got to the Belarus Embassy in St Petersburg where I was applying for my visa. I was travelling on my British passport and had put my initial application in under my British passport. I think if I had used my New Zealand passport I would have got through to Belarus without a problem. But they seemed to be delaying my application, I think because of my British passport. I wasn't organised enough and decided in the end I'd just can it and go to Moscow instead.

MOSCOW

The train from St Petersburg to Moscow was lovely. They actually had places within the train where you could hang up your coats, which I thought was most civilised. The Metro Stations in Moscow were fantastic, beautiful buildings filled with art deco lanterns and tiles. They were mostly built before, during, and soon after World War II. Practically unchanged since their construction, they were susceptible to power cuts and people would get trapped there. Luckily, I didn't! But as pretty as the stations were, it was dreary outside: the sky was overcast and grey.

I'd planned to stay for a short while at a youth hostel that was run by an American. I was amazed at the number of Americans living in Moscow; they were running hostels or working as teachers, although they weren't as well paid as Russian teachers there.

I visited the Red Square in Moscow: the famous city square that separates the Moscow Kremlin, home of the President, from the city's downtown area itself. It was like a spacious flat area amongst the buildings of Moscow near the Kremlin, it was a good place to hang out.

Built in the early fourteenth century, the Kremlin, which means fortress — other cities also have more modest kremlins of their own — overlooks the Moskva (Moscow) River. The Moscow Kremlin, the one that is always meant when people say 'the Kremlin', contains four cathedrals and five palaces. It also contains the world's largest bell, the Tsar Bell, which has never rung, and the world's largest cannon, the Tsar Cannon, which seems to have been fired at least once. They're both ceremonial in reality. They just sit there looking impressive.

I didn't realise it when I was visiting the Kremlin, but I walked right through an area that had been the site of the Battle of Moscow in 1612.

This was a war between Russian and Polish-Lithuanian forces. The Polish-Lithuanian forces were trying to break through the Kremlin. The Russians came out on top and that was the end of that one.

The Kremlin, and Red Square, are flanked by other historically significant structures such as Lenin's Mausoleum and the spectacular multi-turreted building with onion domes made to look like flames dancing, St Basil's Cathedral.

St Basil's Cathedral was built in the 1500s by the first Russian Tsar, Ivan the Terrible, named after his oppressive violent leadership. It is often said that when it was finished Ivan blinded the architect so that its beauty could never be replicated. But that is almost certainly a myth since it is known that the most senior architect in charge of the project continued his practice for some time thereafter!

There were signs everywhere banning visitors from taking photos inside St Basil's, but I couldn't help myself.

The 47 metre high central chapel was breath-taking; the intricate richly-coloured mosaic work was unbelievable. It was completely overwhelming. I'd seen many lavish interiors on my travels but the colours in this one were unlike anything I'd ever seen.

The Bolshoi Theatre opened in 1856 to commemorate Tsar Alexander II's coronation day and is the home of one of the leading ballet companies in the world. It's also on the hundred-rouble banknote, which shows you what a revered institution it is.

Though they didn't have any ballet on while I was there, I did see an opera about Ivan the Terrible. It was four hours long. Even though they had intermissions and English subtitles it was too much! The Bolshoi was a beautiful building though, delicate creams and golds everywhere, with luxuriously-coloured red seating. The interior sparkled.

I did a lot of walking around Moscow. Sometimes the best way to get to know a city well is to just walk around, getting lost and stumbling on places you might otherwise have missed.

Which is exactly what happened to me. I stumbled quite accidentally onto a modern art museum. When I visited, they had a temporary exhibition running on democracy. To anyone reared in the days of the Soviet Union, it was unbelievable and amazing that such a place could exist there now! The museum, one of a total of at least ten modern art museums and galleries in Moscow these days, had some amazing art work that had been donated by a Soviet citizen of Greek parentage called George Costakis.

Born in 1913, Costakis's art collection became the biggest body of modern Russian avant-garde in the world. He conserved all this work that real artists had created in defiance of the Stalin-era preference for stodgy kitsch, and eventually amassed a collection of thousands of officially out-

Figures of smokers at outdoor art museum, Moscow

of-favour paintings, sculptures, and other artworks by early 20th-century artists including Chagall and Kandinsky.

Costakis eventually left the Soviet Union in 1977 for Greece, and donated half of his art to the Tretyakov Museum in Moscow. The rest? He took them with him! They are now mostly in a museum in Greece.

I stumbled across another Museum, an outdoor sculpture one. The sculptures were weird and fantastic. They were all in a garden setting and it reminded me of something similar that had recently started up in Western Park in Auckland, New Zealand. Some of the sculptures were to do with smoking and I tagged two of my friends Nicki Botica and Paul Borich into the image on Facebook and joked with them about it.

I loved Russia. The art, the palaces, the food — it was a memorable trip. I hope to go back again one day, if they will have me.

CHAPTER THIRTY
I Saw Warsaw

THE first thing I noticed is that the international airport was so close to the city centre. The Warsaw Chopin Airport is only ten kilometres away, unlike many major cities that have their international airport far distant, where the land is cheaper.

Opened in 1934 and named after famous composer and resident Frédéric Chopin, Warsaw's international airport has been expanded several times to handle increasing numbers of tourists. It currently processes more than eleven million international passengers a year. Auckland International Airport actually handles more international passengers, but then again there are many short-haul airports in Poland as well, and you can't get to New Zealand by bus or by train.

I landed in the capital on a day commemorating the liberation of Poland from Nazi Germany in 1944. The Warsaw Uprising of 1944, carried out by the Polish Home Army and easily confused with the even more tragic Warsaw Ghetto Uprising of 1943, is famed for being the largest operation carried out by a resistance movement during World War II. The celebrations are intense.

The city was jam-packed; so busy you could hardly move. And at first I just thought it was like this all the time until I realised the significance of the occasion. People were dressed up in 1940s outfits and there were Polish musicians everywhere playing old war songs. It was quite a sight to arrive to!

The Modern Art Museum was a huge disappointment. After all the incredible art in Russia I was expecting more of the same, but this seemed unsophisticated by comparison. I'm sure you wouldn't have to search too far to find some amazing local artists, right?!

I met a retired history teacher from America who showed me around the city. It was moving; actually wandering around the streets where so many Jewish people had been persecuted, with someone who knew the stories inside and out. It was incredible.

He took me to the German-named 'Ghetto': the largest Jewish residential area during Nazi-occupied Europe. A three metre high barbed-wire wall closed off this area to the outside world, and anyone who tried to escape was shot on sight.

Around a quarter of a million residents from this area were sent to extermination camps over a two-month period in 1943. A further one hundred thousand died from starvation and diseases from living in unsanitary conditions caused by their Nazi captors. Before the war there were around three and a half million Polish Jews, the same as the population of New Zealand a generation ago. Ninety per cent of them were killed during the Holocaust.

Warsaw has a tragic history; but there is beauty everywhere. Long cobblestone streets as far as the eye can see and stunning contrasts between restored gothic buildings, cold-war concrete, and modern design. I felt such a mix of emotions here. It's a conflicted and confronting city.

But my trip was coming to an end: it was time to move on. And I headed to Nice in France to visit my good friend Jean-Claude Gomet. The first thing we did was visit a Marc Chagall Museum. I fell in love with his work, and then discovered Chagall was from St Petersburg!

CHAPTER THIRTY-ONE

The Deadliest Mountain in Europe

J EAN-CLAUDE and I planned to climb Mont Blanc, the mountain with the highest fatality rate in Europe. Some estimates say that around a hundred people die each year attempting it: in fact more people lose their lives here each year than in a decade in the Alaskan mountain ranges which are considerably taller and more challenging.

Why is that? Jean-Claude says that the death count here is mostly due to inexperienced and complacent climbers. It's high at 4,808 metres, but not technically a dangerous mountain: it is how you climb it and how well prepared you are that is the issue. Because a tramway takes people part of the way up to the mountain to a teahouse called the Nid d'Aigle or Eagle's Nest at 2,372 metres, located in terrain resembling a ski field, some people think that they can just wander on upwards by themselves.

(This French Eagle's Nest is of course not to be confused with the Kehlsteinhaus in Germany, built at great cost for Adolf Hitler who actually turned out to be too afraid of heights to make much use of it, and which is also now a teahouse.)

A cable car also leads via a quite different route to the Aguille du Midi or 'South Needle' near Mont Blanc at an incredible and much more jagged 3,842 metres. Although only experts are supposed to get off there, anyone can pretend to be an expert I suppose.

It's estimated that with all this artificial assistance, more than twenty

*Mont Blanc Region with access tramway stations and ski runs
visible at top left, Mont Blanc at bottom right, Dôme du Goûter
bottom centre (Google Earth/Satellite, imagery ©Cnes/SpotImage,
DigitalGlobe,Landsat. Map data ©2016 Google)*

thousand people a year attempt to reach the top of Mont Blanc. Among the throng, too many novice climbers are getting into trouble and losing their lives.

Mont Blanc had a lot of rock climbing on ropes and I wasn't confident with knots. But I was still up for the challenge and I knew I'd picked the right person to go with. Jean-Claude had climbed Mont Blanc five times and he worked in an associated industry.

Jean-Claude's job was with a French transport organisation, to help prepare areas for new roads and infrastructure to be built. He worked with climbing and safety on a professional level. He helped to cordon off cliff faces and triggered artificial avalanches to ensure they don't happen naturally. He spends all his time with ropes and helicopters and even though the work is hard, it's well paid. And he gets to climb a lot! Jean-Claude was also a member of the French Alpine Club, one of the best in the world. I couldn't have been in better hands.

We stayed in Chamonix, the site of the first Winter Olympics in 1924, in a place that Jean-Claude has been coming to for years. I'd only ever climbed to a height of less than three thousand metres so far, ironically only a bit higher than the Nid d'Aigle, and this mountain was to be roughly twice as high.

The weather was stunning. At the end of summer the skies are clear and blue, and it's not as busy as other times of the year.

ASCENT

On day one we left from Chamonix to take the tram to the Nid d'Aigle. We were going to be based for a while at the Refuge de Tête Rousse which is usually translated as Tête Rousse Hut though it was really a sort of hostel with catering, and a lot flasher than what most New Zealanders would understand by the word 'Hut'.

The Tête Rousse Hut stands at an altitude of 3,167 metres — which sounds very precise, and must refer to the floor level — next to the small Tête Rousse or 'Redhead' glacier from which it takes its name.

The main thing we needed to do while at Tête Rousse was acclimatise. The height of Mont Blanc required a tiered approach, spending time on various levels and heights to get ourselves used to the lack of oxygen as we ascend.

We followed the routine of short day climbs while based at Tête Rousse: up-stop-down, up-stop-down over a period of five days until we were ready to up-up-up. Again, I suspect that absolute beginners racing up from the teahouse forget that bit, and then conk out further on.

Eventually we had our acclimatisation done and we were ready to climb.

There are three main routes and we were taking the Goûter or Bosses Route to the top, one of the more popular walks because of its (relatively) low difficulty level. There are many routes you can take with different levels of difficulty; I thought the Goûter or Bosses Route would be a good idea for my first ascent of Mont Blanc. This route goes gently up and down by mountaineering standards; it traverses a shoulder of Mont Blanc called the Dôme du Goûter and some smaller bumps called Les Bosses: literally, 'the bumps'.

The mesmerising white glaciers were incredible, and we saw marmots everywhere. They're large squirrels but I think they look more like little wild mountain puppies. They can cause havoc if they get under your car's bonnet: they eat and destroy everything, the local equivalent New Zealand's keas in that respect. Jean-Claude says they're mad for cheese. I guess they're more like giant mice!

While in Tête Rousse we met some interesting people. A lot of them were from Adventure Consultants from New Zealand working as guides on Mont Blanc! It was funny because one guy I met also knew people that I was friends with in New Zealand. I suppose in that sense the climbing community, particularly in New Zealand, is really small.

I told this person about my plans to climb Mount Aspiring in New Zealand's South Island, later that year. Mount Aspiring is located in the Southern Alps of New Zealand and has a height of only 3,033 metres, much lower than Mont Blanc and lower even than Tête Rousse. On the other hand, Mount Aspiring looks like the Matterhorn, a wicked spike pointing into the sky, a more technical proposition than Mont Blanc and with worse and more unpredictable weather to boot. I said I had booked in with a guide named Murray and had already paid my deposit. I was really looking forward to it.

It turned out that Murray had worked in Chamonix. He had even starred in an epic 1988 ski-adventure documentary filmed in Chamonix. Unfortunately, due to the failure of some hired crampons — removable pointy things that are attached to boots to give them more grip on ice — my Mount Aspiring trip was to become an epic of a different sort. More on that later.

One thing I remember quite clearly is the dinner we were served in Tête Rousse Hut. It was bland pasta with cheese and ham and to someone who is gluten intolerant it was horrible. And expensive.

The accommodation and meals cost around $170 per night and that was supposed to include hot showers, but the water was cold. Icy cold. This, after a day climbing, was the opposite of what one needed.

The day of the climb proper, we went up some challenging rocky parts of the route. You could see from the bottom that all the rocks had ropes securely attached on them, which did go to show that people made the effort for the routes to be safe.

That night we stayed in the Goûter Hut, an egg-shaped and futuristic structure which had been built over a twelve year period by the French Alpine Club at 3,835 metres, and was brand new when I was there. It was supposed to be self-sustainable, so everything was running on solar power.

The solar power heated the showers but again, there were no hot showers! Still, the food put on by the caterers here was delicious; maybe it was because I was really hungry.

What I do love about the huts are the people that you meet. We met an Irish couple who were property developers in Ireland. The man had just done Mount Ararat, the highest peak in Turkey and they were planning on climbing Mount Everest together once they were done with Mont Blanc.

We left the Goûter Hut at three a. m. and prepared ourselves for the final ascent to the summit of Mont Blanc. There were about thirty people in our group ready to go. Among them were people from Poland and a group of British Army guys.

I thought Jean Claude was really clever; he had designed and made his own water packs that we could keep close to our bodies. They didn't freeze, even above freezing level. This was actually really important: you could still have a drink from them near the summit and they weren't frozen. That's what really got us to the top. I don't think I would have made it without those packs.

We'd only got about halfway to the top when some of the group started to conk out. We went up through the Dôme du Goûter and over some deep crevasses; it was a very narrow route up. Basically there was only room for two to go through side by side. What really amazed me was the muscly British Army guys began to slow down first and stopped due to exhaustion, before I did!

The last stretch was just in front of us just as dawn was breaking and we made our way up the narrow Bosses Ridge. You had to go single file with a steep drop either side of you. It took us three days to do the Goûter route and make it to the top.

The sunrise was absolutely stunning and it peaked just as we arrived on the summit with the French Alps spread out before you as far as the eye could see. The view of the glaciers from the top was incredible; the green, pink and yellow colours bouncing off different aspects of the glaciers made me feel like I was in a gourmet gelato shop.

We did it. I did it! I made it to the summit of Mont Blanc; I was relieved and proud at the same time.

Of course, climbing Mont Blanc wasn't enough for me, so Jean Claude and I then made plans to next climb the Monte Viso Range in Italy.

CHAPTER THIRTY-TWO
The Stone King

Located in Italy close to the French border a few hours' drive south of Chamonix, Monte Viso *isn't* the highest mountain in the region: but it is famous for looking like a mountainous pyramid. Italians call it colloquially *Il Re de Petra*, the Stone King.

One of the most interesting things about Monte Viso for a New Zealander is that it is the site of a Neolithic jadeite or greenstone quarry, which was used to create things that European museum-keepers call 'cult axes'. These have a striking similarity to objects that Māori also made from greenstone in New Zealand, for the same purpose: that is to say to serve as treasures that would be passed around as tokens of esteem. Woe betide anyone who chipped one by actually using it for any utilitarian purpose!

At one time, it was seriously claimed by some people that Māori were a long lost tribe of Celts or other Europeans, specifically Aryans (ahem), to the point of being actually descended from them by blood.

Notions of this sort, though long since regarded as quite exploded by academics, periodically resurface now and then, often with a whiff of neo-Nazism about them. As with many such theories, the improbability of finding a naturally blonde Māori was not allowed to get in the way of a good, or bad, story; any more than it stopped Heinrich Harrer from looking for his ancestors in Tibet.

The parallelism of the use of greenstone cult axes in Europe and New

Zealand might be read as supporting the idea of an ethnic connection between Europeans and Māori. But again, as with reed boats, you have to be wary about reading too much into this sort of thing.

For, it turns out that cult axes were common in Europe; common in Asia (where Māori originated); common in Africa; and common in the Americas too. And just about everyone made ornaments out of jade or greenstone if they had any as well.

As with reed boats, cult axes can be found everywhere. About all we can say about the affinity between all these various peoples is that they all belong to the human race. And that in any case *ideas*, as well as people, did tend to gradually diffuse around the world in ancient times: particularly so between Europe and Asia, which aren't really all that far apart and largely on the same latitudes.

Wandering tribes find it easier to wander along lines of latitude, where the climate, vegetation and animals may stay pretty much the same, than along lines of longitude where things are more certain to change. And the significance of the wandering tribe is often less that it establishes new bloodlines, which is difficult, than that it brings new ideas and techniques.

Thus Ötzi the five-thousand-year-old Iceman, who was found frozen into a glacier in the Alps in 1991, turns out to have been tattooed at many locations that we would nowadays regard as East Asian acupuncture points corresponding to the ailments he suffered, indeed to the point that there is little doubt that that is what the tattoos were for.

This does not make Ötzi Chinese — scientists can tell that he wasn't — any more than an apparently European cultural practice among the ancestors of the Māori makes them a long-lost tribe of Celts.

It just means that ancient shamans, craft workers and artists were busy pinching each others' best ideas all over Eurasia in the same way that philosophers, musicians and artists have always done; with some of these ideas sometimes being forgotten again, as with acupuncture in Europe. Basically, it is the same as with reed boat parallels.

Returning to the present, we weren't intending to climb Monte Viso, the Stone King, the greenstone-quarry mountain this time: just to hike through the range. I call it tramping in New Zealand, hiking elsewhere!

But first of all, we were going to spend some time exploring the area. I love Italy. The coffee is great (and cheap), good food is inexpensive, and I have lots of friends there that have shown me a local experience rather than the one tourists get.

Land was cheap to buy in this region; and I noticed that there seemed to be an aging population in the area, typical of much of rural Europe. I was astounded to see people still walking around with donkeys or mules, and throughout the mountains there were decaying concrete huts and hidden officers' barracks from the Mussolini era, or earlier perhaps.

After a few days exploring around the Monte Viso region we were ready to hit the mountain.

The Monte Viso range crosses the border between France and Italy; you can see Mont Blanc from its peak. It was quite incredible to see how interlinked Europe actually is. One minute we were in Italy and then the next we were in France. In Italy the peak is known as the Stone King; a quite appropriate name I think given its rocky appearance.

We stayed in a tent while we hiked and one night it got really cold. Jean-Claude and I thought it'd be a good idea to put our sleeping bags together to keep warm. The next morning Jean-Claude was not happy because he didn't get much sleep. I tossed and turned and must have kept him up most of the night! I guess I wasn't used to sharing my sleeping bag.

I was wearing boots I'd bought in Romania, but while using them discovered they were a fraction too small. Big mistake. Not a good thing to do on a long trek. After walking for several days my feet were brutally sore. I don't know how I continued on but I did. I was determined to push on.

In spite of not planning to do any proper climbing, we ended up hiking all the way up to 3,300 metres, just half a kilometre from the top. Even though I was in agony, I'm thrilled that I hiked Monte Viso. It was an amazing adventure!

CHAPTER THIRTY-THREE
Switzerland

I caught the train to Switzerland, a journey I'll never forget: and not for pleasurable reasons. The train was full of criminals. Literally like the film *Con Air*, except this was Con Train. There were handcuffed criminals being transported to Switzerland with forty gendarmes on guard. It was rather intimidating.

I'm not sure what the story was. Maybe the French have regular sweeps of the Swiss Mafia, if there is such a thing: 'Round up the usual suspects'.

I know that police often escort one or two criminals at a time on ordinary planes and trains, but this was excessive. I sat with a woman and tried to avoid what was happening around me. I might be a bit sensitive, but the feeling of being unsafe that the experience gave me never wore off the whole time I was in Switzerland, and spoiled my trip there a bit.

I arrived in the capital, Bern, only to discover that not much was actually run from that city. In contrast to New Zealand, where every decision of any importance is made in Wellington and even a big city like Auckland is micro-managed from afar, Switzerland is made up of twenty-six highly autonomous mini-states called cantons.

Each canton has its own official language; Romansh, German, French or Italian. A few cantons are bilingual and one is even trilingual. And there are numerous dialects. I guess the well-known Swiss neutrality means they've had to placate many neighbours' needs, or arises out of it. I found this fascinating.

All around Bern there are stunning blue ice caves showing signs of where people lived around the last ice age. The underground grottos have become major tourist attractions and that's not surprising; they look like frozen waves and they're below the earth's surface! Incredible.

Switzerland is expensive. A cheap room there cost me nearly $320 a night (and it was of a standard you'd pay under $40 for at a camping ground in New Zealand). On the second night there I heard gunshots from the street: not something I was expecting to hear when I was paying so much!

Despite Bern being a very multicultural city there were signs up everywhere banning the wearing of burqas. MPs voted in overwhelming numbers in 2015 to prevent the country's forty thousand Muslim women from wearing traditional head coverings. Anyone caught wearing one in public will be hit with a $12,000 fine. They say that the burqa ban sends a clear message to fundamentalists. But Amnesty International disagreed and said that it was a sad day for human rights when items of clothing are illegal.

(Interestingly, the same proposal was voted on three years earlier and the majority voted to allow women to wear burqas then.)

I travelled south to Zermatt, the German-speaking area at the foot of the dog-tooth shaped Matterhorn: one of the most famous landmarks in Switzerland and, as I have noted, quite similar to the Mount Aspiring or Tititea that I was so confidently looking forward to climbing in New Zealand.

Most of the local economy in Zermatt is tourism. The resident population of around six thousand swells to many times that during the peak season. Zermatt boasts the highest ski resort in the world, and claims it has more skiable days here than any other place. Their lifts operate 365 days a year so it's a sure bet for a skiing holiday!

The train ride was interesting; filled with international students all travelling to Lausanne to take up their scholarships or to take advantage of low-cost study there. I suspect that the offer of cheaper education was aimed at boosting the numbers of young people there. I heard that because Switzerland has no natural resources, knowledge and education are highly regarded; so their schools are some of the best in the world.

Zermatt is a bustling mountain resort town; there's always something going on and plenty of outdoor exploring to do. It reminded me of Queenstown, except everything was a lot higher up. And Zermatt is an internal combustion-free zone, which helps protect the environment and prevent air pollution. You're only allowed to drive electric cars there, which I loved!

I found a backpacker's hostel for around $50 per night: pretty pricey, but then I'd become used to higher costs in this country.

The Matterhorn has a smaller sibling called the Klein Matterhorn or 'little Matterhorn' in local Swiss German. At 3,883 metres the Klein Matterhorn is still pretty big and its top is in fact the highest point that can be reached by cable car in Europe, and indeed higher than the top of Aoraki / Mount Cook, the highest mountain in New Zealand, a mountain whose old southern Māori name may or may not mean 'cloud piercer'. Return passes up the Klein Matterhorn are expensive; around $75 per adult. But you can get discounted tickets if you go up in the afternoon or off-peak, of course.

I stood at the top of the Klein Matterhorn feeling like a queen surveying her domain. It was beautiful (and I've stood at the top of many mountains).

In spite of the bad start caused by my experience on the train and a few other inconveniences I've mentioned, I loved Switzerland. The architecture had a calming quality to it, and there were oodles of rustic wood chalets everywhere. Many were converted barns with human-families upstairs and cow- families downstairs. Adorable!

CHAPTER THIRTY-FOUR

In the Footsteps of Sir Ed

WITH all this mountaineering going on it's only natural that at some point I'd tackle the biggest mountains, or at least the Base Camp on Mount Everest.

At 8,848 metres, Mount Everest is the tallest mountain in the world. New Zealand-born Edmund Hillary and the Nepalese Tenzing Norgay — a member of the Sherpa people with whom Hillary would later form a strong connection, helping to build hospitals and schools — were the first to climb it. Though how they did it more than sixty years ago in 1953 with the heavy and rudimentary equipment they had is beyond me.

Like most New Zealanders I had grown up with Sir Edmund Hillary being an iconic symbol: he has been the face of our New Zealand five dollar notes for many years. I admire him greatly.

Base Camp is nestled into the side of the mountain and is the starting point for mountaineers attempting the summit. There was a lot of preparation involved: in fact several hours just in presentations.

I would be exploring Nepal over nineteen days with a guide.It was an unbelievable experience. I count myself truly lucky to have been able to do this.

I attempted to be a vegetarian, so that my body would cope better with the high altitudes.

My journey was epic, filled with excitement, fear and love throughout with the most spectacular scenery on the planet.

You can read more about my adventures in Nepal in my book The Maverick Himalayan Way.

But I still have a bit to say about that trip in the next chapter in this book...

CHAPTER THIRTY-FIVE
Holidays Gone Wrong

LIKE every part of life, holidays can also turn to custard. No matter how much you plan, sometimes things are beyond your control. You may get sick, airlines lose your luggage, the hotel or the room isn't what you expected, you get robbed, rooms you've booked and paid for are sold to someone else or you get ripped off. The list is endless.

I've had my fair share of travel disappointments. Where possible, I negotiated and tried to sort out the problem on the spot. Sometimes, I gathered evidence and asked to be compensated but in many situations, I had to let go and move on. Strangely though, in most cases, there was something nice at the end of the disappointment. A silver lining. Here's my list.

STOPPED FROM TRAVELLING TO LHASA

Tibet had been on my travel list for a very long time. I had finally arrived in Kunming, the capital of the Yunnan Province in southwest China, all set to fly to Lhasa in Tibet: but little did I know what awaited me.

A man at the airport (an agent of sorts) informed me that I needed a special permit to visit Tibet. He was talking to a number of Americans who had the same problem and he seemed to be collecting cash off them. It was an organised scam! The Chinese Consulate would approve itineraries, but then add a "new fee" when you arrived in Kunming to pay for an expensive guided tour (that you could only buy off them). It was the only way into Tibet so they had you over a barrel.

I discovered that the Chinese Consulate in New Zealand had to approve my itinerary for both China and Lhasa before I was allowed to travel there, but I was not informed of this until I landed in China. I already had my visa for the country so assumed that this was all I needed.

It was only a three-hour flight to Lhasa from Kunming; I was so close and yet, so far. I'd planned the trip for months and now was turned away for the sake of China's stringent travel policies and out of pocket.

I texted and Skyped with the consulate in Auckland but even now, some years later, I've still not heard anything from them, not even an apology. It's extremely disappointing.

I paid the airport agent $80 for some information, which saved me an unwanted trip to the airport the next morning to try and get to Tibet, and decided to make the best of a bad situation by spending some time in Kunming.

The agent tried to put me up in a grotty hotel by the train station (no doubt he'd earn a commission off it), but I was clear: I was going to stay at the International Youth Hostel.

It turned out to be a great place with good air conditioning. I asked Cynthia, the girl at the hostel to try and get me a refund for my plane ticket to Tibet. She tried for a long time and finally succeeded. I thanked her for her hard work and tipped her as well. Cynthia has been working at the hostel for a while and earns only $430 per month. She was lovely and wanted me to like China.

And like China, I did!

The ancient limestone caves about ninety kilometres southeast from Kunming were a treat. Many of them are lit beautifully, so it felt like I was walking inside a rainbow.

But the real highlight was the Yunnan Nationalities Museum, a tribute to the dozens of ethnicities that lived in the province. I saw a stunning two-hour performance by the Kunming minorities that reminded me of the Samoan drummers in New Zealand: I felt like I was at Auckland's Polyfest (the Pacific Island Festival!) Of course this might have something to do with the fact that Polynesians are related to certain Asian minorities. What also impressed me was that a lot of the artwork and masks were also very similar to ones I'd seen in Thailand, India and Nepal.

But sadly, not everyone appreciated the performance. Members of the Communist Party were given free tickets, and before the performance ended they refused to applaud like the rest of us. Instead, they all stood up together in formation and left — in formation. Around two hundred and fifty of them. All in uniform. It was bizarre and very disrespectful. Especially, as the shows were world-class.

But that wasn't my last dealing with Communist Party weirdness.

I was in the hostel and I saw a man dressed in uniform scowling and smoking through the main lobby area. Usually I would say something to an indoor smoker ("take it outside") but as he was a stern-looking soldier I kept my distance. He shouted at the female cleaners.

After he left I asked the women what he'd said. They replied in surprisingly good English for such a remote location; "Clean the windows!"

Apparently, he's obsessed with the cleanliness of the windows in Kunming and comes here regularly to complain about the cleaning job. The women said they'd deliberately leave a mark on the window so that when he came back he'd shout again.

They'd stifle their laughter, leaving it until well after he'd left!

Sure enough, two days later the same sulking, smoking communist soldier marches through the hostel inspecting windows. Everything appears to his liking until he spots a mark. He started yelling at a volume and pace that shocked me. The girls' stony faces and slightly bowed heads (for respect) conveyed nothing but remorse. After he left they chuckled to themselves. And, reiterated to me that his eruptions amused them.

I ended up loving Kunming. Not only did I have a rich cultural experience, but there was fantastic street food. Everywhere I turned there was fresh, tasty, flavoursome and cheap food. I was in gastronomic barbecue heaven.

HEAT AND DIRT IN INDIA

It was my first visit to India — something I'd always looked forward to. But when I arrived in New Delhi, it was fifty degrees and there was a city-wide power cut. I couldn't even get money out. With no air conditioning working anywhere I felt like I was in hell, such was the heat.

I was staying in an area where backpackers live. On the first day, I saw a man crapping on the street outside my hotel! Right there in the street, in full view of everyone, but that wasn't even the worst of it. The drains on the street were open and dirty, plus the nearby public toilet was overflowing and smelt like hot sewage. Even the local people held their noses as they walked past the area. It was vile. And not a great start to my Indian adventure.

As nice as the people at the hotel were, my room wasn't quite what I had expected. I had a strong feeling that there would be rats everywhere at night. So, I moved to a different hotel. It was an improvement on the previous hotel but I took one look at the kitchen and decided I couldn't eat there. I would definitely get sick. I finally figured out that the best way to find good restaurants was to ask the locals. I would often walk up to a well-dressed Indian man or woman and ask them where they ate, and go to the same restaurant. That worked.

Another mistake I made was going to a government tourist agency. The people in my hotel had recommended that I go to the tourism department offices and ask them to organise my tour. I followed their advice and booked and paid for a multi-stop tour with them.

My first stop five hours south in Jaipur was nice, but very hot and full of tourist agents who nagged me to go with them to a hotel, restaurant, shopping district or even sightseeing - so they could earn their commission. It was quite stressful and I had to constantly tell people to leave me alone. I just ended up yelling at anyone who tried to bother me that they should clear off (only more forcefully put). It seemed to work.

I rode an elephant to the Amber Fort, which was interesting. A former Raja had painted everything pink or red, so the colourful Iranian-made forts that had been there since the 13th century made for a delightful journey on the back of the world's biggest land animal. I like riding elephants: the jerkiness of their shoulders moving makes you feel like you're on a gentle rollercoaster.

I went to the Galtaji Temple, also known as the Monkey Temple, outside Jaipur city. There are over a hundred monkeys there. Some of them can be quite aggressive and I almost smacked one of them who tried to grab my camera!

I was supposed to travel on an overnight train from Calcutta to Sikkim, and a guide was helping me with the transfers: it was all part of the $1,600 tour price I'd paid. The Calcutta railway station was filthy (absolutely disgusting) and there were people sleeping on the floor, and not just because the train was running late; it looked like people lived on the train station floor.

Then I found out that I had a second-class ticket. There was no way I was going to travel second class in an Indian train. No, don't get me wrong. A lot of people travel in these trains and there's nothing wrong with it. I was just afraid that I would fall sick with the heat and dust. I have to admit, I was also a bit afraid of the toilets. I asked my guide to take me to a hotel and told him I was not going to take the train. The guide kept asking me for money all the way to the hotel.

At one point I had to firmly tell him that I was not going to give him any money and that he should get it from the government travel agency in New Delhi. They had arranged my trip and as I'd pre-paid everything they were responsible for paying him. Later I did a Google search on the travel agency and found that they had over thirty bad reviews!

The next day I took a flight to Bagdogra en route to Sikkim. As we were driving through the mountains we were stopped at a checkpoint, well before our arrival destination of Gangtok.

The checkpoint was a place where foreigners had to register before entering Sikkim. The customs guard checked my passport and said I had no visa for India on my passport. I told him that I had a visa on arrival and tried to explain what it meant and how it was different from the regular tourist visa. But he didn't seem to know anything about arrival visas. I was surprised that the visa policies were not communicated to customs officers in areas far away from New Delhi.

I was detained at the checkpoint for over two hours and I thought I would soon get arrested.

Finally, my taxi driver came in and spoke to the customs guard and he let me go. Later, I found out that I could have taken an inexpensive helicopter to the Bagdogra airport and it would have saved me all this trouble.

RIPPED OFF IN NEPAL

The devastating earthquake in 2015 caused havoc throughout Nepal. More than eight thousand people died and hundreds of thousands of families were displaced. Villages were flattened and the earthquake triggered an avalanche on Mt Everest killing twenty-one people, making it the deadliest day ever on the mountain.

It wasn't my first time to Nepal. The last time I had trekked to the Everest Base Camp and Manaslu Base Camp, below the eighth highest mountain in the world. I had spent two months submerged in the culture and it was a once-in-a-lifetime experience. So many incredible things happened.

During one of my visits I left the Base Camp and visited the colourfully-attired Kalash people, who long claimed to be the descendents of a lost outpost of Alexander the Great's army. Recent DNA testing, which is fast clearing up so many mysteries, suggests that they are actually descended from Siberian hunter-gatherers. All the same this was remarkable.

But this trip was mostly about expressing my solidarity with the people who were struggling to recover from the disaster, by being a tourist and spending money there.

I had booked a tramp through Mahendra, a trekking company guide and owner of the company.

I was to climb the Lobuche and Island peaks but on arriving in Kathmandu, I discovered the trek was cancelled. I was disappointed and found other trekkers who had similar problems. I managed to get my money back so I booked on another trip, this time with the International Sherpa Adventure run by Nuru Jangbu Sherpa.

The cost was a whopping $7,600 that was supposed to include everything – all the fees for two peaks, insurance for the guides, food and accommodation while on the trek.

I wasn't comfortable with the company keeping my passport: but I was assured by them (and other travellers) that it was pretty standard practice here. I did receive it back after the trip.

I travelled by jeep to Jiri to begin my trek. I had a porter named Mr. Limbu and a climbing guide called Chaturang. Unfortunately, as it turned out, Chaturang was not really interested in my itinerary and told me I had to choose between the peaks and the passes because we couldn't do both.

This was maddening because I wasn't informed about this change in itinerary when I paid for the trek. I tried to get my money back and withdraw but the company rules did not allow withdrawals.

For the next three weeks I was stuck with a guide who was not interested in taking me to the peaks. In fact, Chaturang also questioned my mountaineering skills and said I didn't know how to use an ice axe or crampons and he would not risk his life for me. But I was experienced in using them both! I'd done three mountaineering courses and had used them many times over the last five years.

The passes were absolutely beautiful and I had a great view of the Lobuche peak — a razor-sharp mountain slicing the blue sky — but my guide refused to take me further up. I couldn't understand why; it wasn't a difficult climb (non-technical mountain people go up it all the time). Many of the lives lost in the previous year's avalanche were Sherpas, and I suspect that his feelings had something to do with the general resentment building within the Sherpa community.

Another problem was the poor-quality hotels I was staying in. Chaturang had booked me into dirty hotels infested with rats. Since the company was paying for the hotels, they wanted me to go to the cheapest place. But often I put my foot down and insisted on cleaner places. At one point Chaturang even tried to restrict my Internet usage, making it difficult to check in on my property business.

One of the most important things I've found when travelling is having a valid SIM card in every country you are travelling in; I even had one in Kashmir. This has come in handy for me more than once!

On the way I met two young guys who had done Lobuche. They had gone with a different company. I wished I had gone with their trekking company. When I reached Kathmandu, I managed to get a small refund but it was a sad experience and I felt I had been ripped off.

I complained to the New Zealand Consulate but they refused to help saying they couldn't get involved in 'civil disputes'.

BOOKED (BUT NOT BOOKED) IN KANAZAWA, JAPAN

Sometimes, hotel bookings turn out to be a bad experience. I've heard of travellers who have booked online and paid for hotels that didn't exist. Others have spoken of hotels that look nice online but when you actually see your room; it's a completely different picture. I've booked and had to stay in bad hotels sometimes: but I've tried to quickly check out and move to better places. Of all places in the world, I had a booking fiasco in Japan.

This was my second trip and I was on my way from Kyoto to Hakuba in the Japanese Alps, the home of the 1998 Nagano Olympics. I was organised and knew I'd be staying the night at Kanazawa so I'd pre-booked a mixed dorm bed at the Good Neighbours Hostel. The reviews were quite positive and the location looked good: close to the train station.

However, when I arrived, the people at the hostel insisted they had no booking for me. I tried to convince them I had but it didn't work. Instead, they tried to charge me $100 to access my room!

Boat Ride on the Dal (City Lake), Srinagar, Kashmir

In Tenboche, with Mount Everest in the background

Woman gathering water lilies, important for traditional medicines and other uses on the Dal, Srinagar, Kashmir

In Tenboche, with Mount Everest in the background

From what I could gather, hostel.com took their fee and I never got a refund. I tried to argue with the people at the hostel and convince them that I had indeed paid for a bed, but soon decided it was not worth it. I went online and quickly booked a place on Airbnb and I ended up having an amazing stay. My host picked me up from the bus station and took me to a traditional Japanese inn just outside Kanazawa. I slept on tatami mats, admired the bonsai garden, swam in the hot pools and enjoyed great food in local restaurants. I was celebrated there because I was the only non-Japanese person in a non-touristy part of Japan. I felt like a rock star!

The Great Wall, China

PAKISTAN TREK FAIL

In July 2014 I was in Pakistan, trekking around the Rosh Gol Glacier in the Hindu Kush Mountains. I was part of a team with Patricia Deavoll, one of New Zealand's top mountaineers who had climbed over thirty-seven peaks in three decades. She and her climbing partner Chris Todd were to trek to the 6,827 metre high mountain Languta-e-Barfi on the border of Afghanistan and Pakistan, and my climbing partner David and I had to decide where we wanted to go.

One of the most important aspects of trekking is to have the right climbing partner. I was climbing with David, who I'd only just met. I thought he'd be great. He wasn't.

Patricia says that picking the right person to climb with ensures safety and survival, if things go wrong. But then most climbers know that. The last thing you want on a mountain in bad weather is somebody that you don't trust or that doesn't know what they're doing.

From the very onset, it was clear that David and I had our differences. On reaching the base camp, while we were preparing for the trek, David sat around reading. Five days went by and then, finally we went to a nearby valley to practise some of our mountaineering skills and I found that I wasn't very good with the ropes. Ropes have never been my strong point, unfortunately.

On the other hand I'd just been in Nepal, so I was in peak climbing mode in both senses of the word 'peak'. David was unfit. So, travelling with him was frustrating.

We had agreed that we would climb up to 4,800 metres and camp so that the next day we could go up to 1,500 metres and head back down. Unfortunately, David changed the plan unilaterally and decided to go ahead and camp at a different place. It didn't feel good. David had no respect for me and it was difficult for me to trust him and go ahead. He reached the top ahead of me and then rushed down saying it was too far and that I shouldn't bother. I didn't listen to him and went ahead to the top by myself.

I decided I couldn't risk my life any longer and waste more of my time. Besides, I was carrying a very heavy tent and David hadn't brought my bivvy bag — a waterproof fabric bag which can be used as improvised shelter, a vital piece of survival equipment anywhere that's cold, wet or windy — so I thought it was better to head back to the base camp instead of forging ahead. David, of course, never forgave me for this. But it's a decision I made for my safety and I have no regrets about it.

My time at the base camp turned out to be interesting though; just spending time with so many people from all over the world made me feel like part of a small Everest community.

I loved it. Despite the obstacles.

* * *

As a traveller, you too will encounter uncertainties and disappointments along the way. I've learned that each disappointment taught me important lessons. And so, I've learned to embrace the situations and move on.

CHAPTER THIRTY-SIX

The Worst. Just the Worst.

AFTER doing a few snow craft courses I was keen to climb Mount Aspiring, the so-called Matterhorn of the South. As I really understood the importance of having a trustworthy climbing partner, not least on a technical climb like Mount Aspiring, I decided to stay safe by hiring a guide.

A well-known expert solo mountaineer had recommended that I get in touch with an equally well-known alpine guide named Murray, the legend of Chamonix. I spoke with Murray about climbing Mount Aspiring and he was very optimistic from the get-go, saying that if I were a 'fit kiwi tramping chick' then I would get to the top of the mountain no problem.

The contract was on the usual basis, for Mount Aspiring, of a five-day window to allow for changeable weather and more than one summit attempt.

I was so eager to do the climb and so confident that I would indeed get to the top in one day that I made a down-payment well in advance. Thus began a sequence of events that led to me not getting to the top.

A rolling snowball of fiasco began to take shape when I discovered that I had left my own crampons in storage in Auckland. Down south, I hired a pair from a local sporting-and-outdoors shop. But leaving my crampons behind wasn't a good omen, in view of the vulnerability of a one-day trip to things going wrong. And the prophecy would soon be fulfilled.

In December 2013, Murray and I flew to the Bevan Col landing site by helicopter, put up our tents for the first night and went to bed early, for we had an early start the next day. We got up at four a.m. and walked across the Bonar Glacier to Colin Todd Hut, a distance of about two and a half kilometres, in crampons.

After only ten minutes of progress across the glacier, one of my crampons failed. Ten minutes after that, the other one failed!

When we got to the Colin Todd Hut, Murray repaired both my crampons with wire. But by the time the repairs were complete, at half past eight in the morning, he judged that the weather was now too bad to attempt a safe ascent. At the Colin Todd Hut, another guide told me I could still get to the top.

All the same, Murray judged that it would not be prudent to continue and in fact cancelled the whole five-day expedition and offered me a partial refund.

We left Bevan Col at five p.m. by helicopter and the following day I returned to the shop to raise the issue of the failed crampons. I was fuming. I was annoyed with Murray for cancelling and not being prepared to wait it out, but I also felt that it was the failure of the crampons which had ultimately put the kibosh on things.

I left Steve, the manager of the store, my mobile number to make contact but heard nothing from him regarding reparations. I spoke to the lobby group Outdoors New Zealand and laid a work safety complaint with the Ministry of Business, Employment and Innovation.

I also laid a complaint with the Disputes Tribunal to try and get back some or all of my outstanding costs for helicopter hire and guide fees. My guide fees were still substantial even if, in the circumstances, Murray was not going to charge for the whole five days. Nor did the helicopter come cheap.

On top of that there was the crampon hire fee, although that was a pittance compared to helicopter and guide.

An article was published in the Southland Times and on the news website www.stuff.co.nz about the incident (Debbie Jamieson, 'Would-be climber alarmed hired crampons fell apart' 11 December 2013), in which both Murray and the shop manager downplayed the seriousness of the situation.

Murray claimed that the crampon failure was not life- threatening as the crampons came apart before we got onto the main part of the climb, and that if they were going to fail due to some defect it would have been normal for them to fail early in the day before we really got going.

As, indeed, they did.

All the same I had been on the Bonar Glacier when it happened. Without crampons, I could still have slipped and perhaps fallen into a crevasse in a worst-case scenario, even if it wasn't as dangerous as the later stages of the climb.

And while Murray thought the crampons might have come apart because they were getting a bit worn and tired — this does happen — Steve insisted there was nothing wrong with the crampons, going so far as to say they had been "misused."

In any case, both Steve and Murray put most of the blame on me. Steve complained to the news media that "People get out of their depth and go up into the mountains. I don't know what sort of climber she is." Murray also dismissed me in print as a tramper rather than a mountaineer.

(Actually, I had just been up Mont Blanc.)

Postscript: My complaint with the Disputes Tribunal was ultimately heard a bit over a year later, in January 2015. The Tribunal did not direct either Murray or Steve to repay anything further toward the cost of my helicopter flights and guide fees. I did get the cost of crampon hire back, though!

CHAPTER THIRTY-SEVEN

An Active Xmas

I T was Christmas time and it wasn't going to exactly be the relaxing Christmas break I was after.

Kahurangi National Park is the second largest national park in New Zealand after Fiordland. With over five hundred and seventy kilometres of tracks, including the famous seventy-eight kilometre Heaphy Track, Kahurangi is tramping heaven. With its coastal palm forests, marble mountains, rare birds like the rock wren and the spotted kiwi, and tussock high country, it's an incredible place to be.

In Māori Kahurangi means treasured possession, which is exactly what this park is. For hundreds of years the Māori used tracks through this region to find greenstone, called pounamu in Māori, which they used for prized jewellery passed down from one generation to the next.

It rained heavily and there were gale-force winds, reaching speeds of up to eighty knots: strong enough to blow your boots off if you weren't careful. But even though the weather was wild, the huts were stunning: the most diverse that I have ever seen.

There were ladders leading to platforms sheltered under rocky overhangs, huts nestling in caves, old gold miners' quarters and even a restored 'love shack' with a built-in fireplace.

Part of the Kahurangi National Park, the Cobb Valley can be accessed from the Upper Takaka district, at the base of the Takaka Hill along thirty-eight kilometres of unsealed road. Mount Arthur, the principal mountain in the area, can be reached via the Graham Valley Road, thirty-five kilometres from Motueka. Access to the Nelson Tablelands, a high plateau, can be gained on foot via each of these two routes, and the west coast of the South Island can be reached from the Leslie- Karamea Track.

There are no major unbridged rivers to cross in this area and Mount Arthur does not have the sort of high, narrow ridges from which you could fall to your death — so for me a relatively hazard free trip!

I took Eleanor Catton's *The Luminaries* with me as reading material and it was great to have a story about West Coast gold miners to read as I traversed a track rich with the same landscapes and history.

The diverse terrain I covered included a series of unique geological features. Mt Arthur is made of hard, crystalline marble: below the ground are some of the deepest shafts and most intricate cave systems in the world. Cavers have currently joined two cave systems in the area and made a massive thirty-six kilometre long, twelve hundred metre deep underground labyrinth. Nettlebed is now the deepest cave in the Southern Hemisphere.

In contrast, the Tablelands are made of limestone and quartz that were lifted and twisted over millennia to form mountains. The Cobb Valley is different again: its rivers were once glaciers smoothing and polishing the rock as they advanced to form a U-shaped valley, always the sign of a now-vanished glacier as opposed to the steep V that is carved by a river. The valley today still bears many signs of its former glaciers and is filled with volcanic rock, schist and sandstone.

I started my trip with a thirty minute walk up to Flora Hut. During the 1870s gold was discovered in the area and the diggers used to pitch their tents on these plains. Most of the workers were paid by the government to pan for gold, but little was found. It was one of the first unemployment schemes in New Zealand: but due to the lack of 'colour' as miners used to say in those days — the colour in question being yellow and shiny — operations disbanded by the 1880s.

Another hour's walking and I'd reached the Mount Arthur Hut, the first stop on the way to ascending the highest peak in the Kahurangi Park, Mount Arthur (1,795 metres) itself.

However, I met a father and son who, though they had made it to the top, were quick to warn me about the poor visibility and low cloud they'd encountered. With this news and the torrential rain, I decided to wait it out and make my attempt the following day.

I awoke the next morning and waited until eleven a.m. for the weather to improve. By eleven it was clear but the high winds still remained. I knew it would take me about two to three hours to reach the summit and the winds were reaching speeds of eighty knots. Luckily, I had just got myself a Personal Locator Beacon and as far as I could judge there were no major ridges on the ascent. After weighing up my options I decided I would wait for gaps in the wind gusts and cloud cover and dash up as best I could. After two hours, I'd made it to the signposts. It was rather slow going. The first peak still looked a bit iffy with lurking clouds that would potentially hinder my visibility.

But in life everything is a risk and so I continued. As I'd hoped, the clouds lifted and I attained the first peak!

Next up was Winter Peak. I still had a long way to go and I was hampered by navigating schist and deep holes in the rock. Needless to say, I took it slowly: I did not want to risk falling down one of those crevasses!

I eventually made the peak and wow, what a view! A barren, marvellous landscape riddled with caves. I almost got blown off the top of the mountain though, so I only spent a minute there before slowly heading back down to the hut. I became an expert at leaning back into the weight of my pack to stop myself being blown away. Due to the low cloud, I only saw the Nelson plains and not the rest of the view I'd been hoping for. But it was still magic.

I stayed the night in Mount Arthur Hut again. Amazingly, there were only two people there each night which was great; I was expecting it to be busier this time of the year.

The next morning I was ready to head out again. I wanted to experience the sunrise with the kea, bellbirds and warblers for company. I decided to avoid all major rain and so headed to a lower elevation, aiming for Asbestos Cottage or 'the Love Shack' as I call it. Little did I know, I was about to see what I now consider to be the most interesting hut in New Zealand.

I dropped back down to Flora Hut, and then followed the Flora Stream through to the Upper Gridiron and the Gridiron Shelter.

The Gridiron Hut is very quaint in appearance. It's tucked under a rock, practically inside the mouth of a cave. Though the hut only sleeps four there is also an adjoining outdoor camping area. At the nearby Lower Gridiron Shelter, there's a ladder leading to a platform that can sleep eight. It reminded me of a structure I'd seen in Takaka. After exploring the sleeping areas at Gridiron I headed on for another two and half hours to Asbestos Cottage.

What a blast from the past this place is!

It was built in 1897 by people searching for asbestos in the area. Back then asbestos was used for its fire-retardant and insulating properties and was used widely in civil and mechanical engineering. Pipe-lagging and the insulation of boilers were classic uses. But now we know that asbestos is a carcinogen that causes mesothelioma, a rare, fatal lung cancer that is nearly always associated with exposure to asbestos; as well as other lung diseases of the wheezy, obstructive sort that can have a range of causes, asbestos included.

A combination of exposure to asbestos *and* smoking multiplies the assault on the lungs exponentially. And of course, most people smoked as well back in the old days: especially tough manual workers who spent all day around steam-pipes and the like.

In 1914, Annie Fox moved into the remote Asbestos Cottage after fleeing her abusive husband with her two teenage sons and her lover, Henry. The family were largely self-sufficient: they grew vegetables and fruit from their impressive garden and Henry and the boys hunted deer and goat. To make money they panned for gold and extracted asbestos from rocks, but that wasn't very lucrative. To help make ends meet, they took rainfall readings for the Meteorological Service for twenty-nine years. The couple lived there for nearly forty years as virtual recluses. When Henry died Annie moved to Timaru to be with her sister. But she missed the solace of the area and ended up taking her own life.

Stepping into the tiny 7.6 by 3.6 metre cottage is like going back in time; it's still the same as it was a hundred years ago when Annie and her family lived there. The same old chairs are still resting places for tired behinds. The same fireplace still warms the feet of cold trampers. And visitors even discovered a few bottles of Henry's moonshine!

I slept very well in the cottage, amidst the history and the continuing rain. I would have liked to stay longer but I wanted to finish my adventure and see the rest of this beautiful, varied backcountry track. There are many images of the Gridiron shelters and of Asbestos Cottage available online, far more than I could show here.

On leaving Asbestos Cottage my plan was to cross Peat Flat, traverse Peel Ridge, pass alongside Mount Peel and head out onto the Tablelands, ending the day at Balloon Hut.

This was an eight-hour tramp, complete with the ever-present eighty-knot wind, and I had to put on all of the winter gear I'd packed. In one day, I passed through a staggering array of landscapes. Peat Ridge was half clad in bush and half in tussock. This was followed by beech forest. And then, on the slopes of Mount Peel, I made my way over schist and limestone.

The first Balloon Hut was built in 1909 and went on to house a melting pot of miners, hunters, trampers and skiers. A mine once operated on Mount Peel, and you can still see the old tracks the miners used. In the winter, back-country skiers continue to make use of the hut.

In 1995, almost a hundred years after it was first built, the Waimea Tramping Club rebuilt Balloon Hut. It is now a serviced, modern-day hut that can sleep fourteen people.

On my final day in the park I walked from Balloon Hut across the Tablelands to Salisbury feeling invigorated and impressed that I'd risen to my own challenge.

CHAPTER THIRTY-EIGHT

Can't Get Enough of the Irish Charm

I have a British passport, so spending time travelling around the United Kingdom and Europe has always been hassle-free for me (no visas or travel restrictions in place). Although what that will mean now with Brexit, who knows?!

I was heading back to Ireland again to stay with my good friends Ina and John. And we were off to visit the Blasket Islands together.

The Islands known as *Na Blascaodaí* in Irish are a chain of six islands off the west coast of the country. The islands were was abandoned in 1953 because of a declining population; young people left to find work and there were only twenty-two inhabitants left. Even at the peak there were only 175 people there, living self-sufficiently far from medical services. Islanders were unaffected by the Potato Famine in the mid-1800s. They weren't entirely dependent on potatoes, and their crops weren't ravaged like elsewhere around Ireland.

The most westerly point in Europe, the Blasket Islands are now purely a tourist destination. With over a thousand acres or more than four square kilometres of unspoilt mountainous terrain overlooking the ocean on Great Blasket Island, as well as five smaller islands, the Blaskets have become a thriving place for flora, fauna and tourists.

There are still no permanent residents here though — the village on Great Blasket is like a ghost town — but tourists can book into the five available restored self-catering houses.

We stayed at a gorgeous rustic abandoned house and strolled around the island noticing how many other houses were discarded and in a state of disrepair. It wasn't the best catch-up trip with my friends, I felt like an awkward third wheel. Then they both got tick bites! I was so used to being in tick-rich environments that I always tucked my trousers into socks and wore a hat. But my friends were itchy (and scratchy).

Even so, the islands were beautiful and it was unusually warm there.

CARRAUNTOOHIL

I'd often thought about climbing the highest mountain peak in Ireland; it's apparently one of the best hikes to do in the country.

At 1,038 metres high, Carrauntoohil wasn't going to be as taxing as some of the other climbs I'd done. We were taking Ina's twelve year-old daughter with us, so we decided to take a guide to make sure we were on the right path for the fourteen-kilometre, six-hour journey.

We started from a place called Cronin's Yard: the traditional starting point for over three centuries. It is a majestic beginning. The countryside gives way to a pyramid-shaped mountain and the rolling green hills are intercepted by rocky valleys. It's beautiful. It reminded me of the Canterbury Plains in New Zealand's South Island. Apparently this area was once covered in forest,but the Irish and their later English overlords harvested the timber and cleared the area for farming purposes.

After the hike was over I headed up to Burren, or the Burren as it is colloquially known — the littlest national park in Ireland. At only fifteen square kilometres, it is small but perfectly formed. There are fresh-water springs, woodlands, petrified forests, grasslands and rocky cliff faces: it's a veritable feast for the eyes.

I also discovered giant stone tombs in a stunning outdoor museum, some of which were ten thousand years old! They're a bit like Stonehenge in their design: but they are stand-alone monuments, rather than in a circle. Like Stonehenge, no-one knows how they were constructed, especially with roof stones weighing around one hundred tonnes. But experts have surmised that a combination of wooden rollers, ropes, animals and earth-ramps were used to put them together. There are close to two hundred of these around the Burren: it's like being in The Flintstones. One of the excavated tombs revealed twenty-two people (sixteen adults and six children), so unlike the mystery of Stonehenge we know why they were constructed.

Burren is also famous for rare Irish species of plants, some of which are only found in the area. Forty years ago an organic perfumery started here using native flowers to make perfumes, creams, soaps and balms.

LONDON (AGAIN...)

After the Burren I headed to London for a short stop and what a change from my last visit a decade ago! The food was delicious: gone were the stodgy pub-type establishments and in their place were fresh food eateries! London had finally caught up with New Zealand standards.

I loved the Camden Markets in North London, a vibrant and diverse group of alternative shops and stalls next to the canal. Opened in the 1970s, the markets have become a popular tourist destination with around one hundred thousand people visiting each weekend. It's also where punk exploded. In 1966 Pink Floyd played their first gig here. Others who have performed in the area are the The Sex Pistols, The Clash, The Damned and Chrissie Hynde. The Clash's debut album cover was shot in Camden. And famous punk designer Vivienne Westwood has a watch in her collection called the Camden Lock, named after the device used to lower and raise watercraft on the canal.

The punk subculture is still alive and well in Camden even though the area has become more commercialised. To prove that point, for £1 you can have your photo taken with punk rockers at the Camden Market: so I did! Being in the punk epicentre made me feel like I'd come full circle since my punky rebellious teen years. Although, I'm still a maverick.

CHAPTER THIRTY-NINE
Scotland

I left London and flew north to Edinburgh; the home of the Fringe Festival, the largest arts festival in the world. It was created to celebrate culture in the area and cheer everyone up after World War II.

In 2015, there were more than 50,000 performances in 313 venues; a far cry from its humble beginnings in 1947 when eight theatre groups showed up to the more respectable Edinburgh International Festival, begun in the same year, without proper invitation or selection and decided to organise a festival of their own on the fringes of the 'proper' festival.

I loved the fringe festival. One of the first acts I saw was a young comedian talking about ayahuasca (also known as iowaska), the revolting-tasting hallucinogenic tea I'd drunk in Ecuador. It's legal in South America but illegal in the West.

He joked about how they'd boiled and drunk it and almost immediately vomited and had explosive bouts of diarrhoea. I laughed so hard because exactly the same thing happened to me!

After he'd finished his story, he asked the audience whether anyone there had tried it. Stupidly, I put my hand up and was grilled by him. Everyone laughed, but I was embarrassed and kept saying defensively that it was legal where I'd taken it!

* * *

I'd always loved Edinburgh Castle and so do others. It's Scotland's most popular tourist attraction. Every year nearly two million people file through the gates; gates that my grandmother used to swing on as a little girl growing up nearby.

Built in the twelfth century, the world-famous landmark has housed everything from royals to soldiers and ammunition to accused witches awaiting trial and execution within its walls. It used to be much smaller. Renovations and expansions in the fifteenth and sixteenth century and even a touch-up after World War One have turned it into the grand building that we see there today.

While wandering through the castle's impressive rooms and halls I overhead some French people asking why signs were in French. I told them that Mary Queen of Scots, who became queen as an eight-day old baby after her father King James V of Scotland died, was smuggled at just five years of age out of Scotland to France to her mother's homeland, and lived there until she was eighteen. So, Mary Queen of Scots was French too!

Even though the Gaelic language is semi-indigenous to Scotland — having been brought over by Irish Gaels a long time ago, so that it quite closely resembles Irish — it is spoken by only one per cent of the population. Scots Gaelic is spoken by less than sixty thousand people, and that number is dropping rapidly. Ten years ago, nearly twice as many people were fluent. Part of Gaelic's decline was due to it being banned by the English in 1746 along with tartan and bagpipes. It has really only been revitalised in the last thirty years with a number of programmes aimed at introducing younger speakers to the language. I do hope that the Scots succeed with the Gaelic revival. I would hate for it to become extinct.

DUNDEE

I'd heard that Dundee had changed a lot in the seven years since I'd been last, so I headed an hour north to catch up with my Aunty June.

We started going through her mother's (my grandmother's) things and we came across my grandmother's birth certificate, which listed her first address, only 90 minutes south in Leith. I couldn't *not* go.

I hired a car and went to visit my gran's home. We had a very close relationship. She used to spend weekends with us in Hastings, New Zealand, so I'd grown up knowing her and going to see her old home was very emotional and nostalgic for me. When I got there I realised I'd been by the house before; I'd actually randomly walked past her house seven years ago when I was last in the area!

I could imagine the era she was born into at the turn of the century. She'd had a hard life and had grown up surrounded by coalmines and jute mills. Even though her family were comfortable financially, she was disowned at the age of fifteen for reasons that I don't know.

I always enjoy Aunty June's company; she's full of life. But I wasn't expecting her to be so lively that she'd join me climbing Ben Nevis, the United Kingdom's tallest mountain! I hadn't planned to climb another mountain just yet, but thought what the heck: I'm in the area and my Aunty June will come with me. It'll be fun!

My Aunty June borrowed some second hand tramping boots, which is never advisable because boots need to fit properly and they need to be worn in. Her sons (my cousins) were not happy because they viewed it as too challenging for a 75-year-old. But her lust for life is one of the reasons why she's still so vibrant. They eventually conceded because they thought we'd do the less difficult route, the touristy bit that fat people did. But we didn't.

Ben Nevis is only three hundred metres higher than Carrauntoohil which I climbed in Ireland, but it has some of the steepest cliff faces in the United Kingdom as well, making parts of it really difficult to climb.

We started walking to the summit of Ben Nevis. After only one hour of walking Aunty June's borrowed boots broke. She begged other walkers for tape and temporarily fixed them. But that didn't last long. Aunty June had to stop; there was no way her boots would get her up to the summit and I wanted to push on. Aunty June was quite disappointed that she didn't make it up, but it would have been dangerous (and painful) for her to continue.

I was glad that I'd taken all of my wet weather gear with me. Thank God I did. When we reached the summit, it was freezing. We were greeted by torrential rain and I had to put on all my woollen and wet weather gear. I was so happy that I had insisted on taking it with me.

After we made it back down to Fort William, Aunty June hopped on a bus back to Dundee, and I headed to Kinlochleven to do the West Highland Walkway.

Kinlochleven was built just over a century ago for the sole purpose of housing workers from the nearby hydro-electric plant and aluminium smelter (the largest in Europe at the time). And it was the first village in the world in which every home was connected to electricity: it's still sometimes called the Electric Village. The smelter closed down due to its outdated equipment: new factories being built could process the ore more efficiently. Over time the population dropped and now there are only around a thousand residents.

But new business ventures have kept Kinlochleven in business. The West Highland Walkway attracts more than 85,000 walkers each year and the National Ice Climbing Centre has been a boost to tourism.

I set up my tent by some ruins near a stream. It was an idyllic spot. But not for long. I headed down to the stream to get water for a cup of tea and when I opened my mouth thousands of midges flew in! It reminded me of being on a motorbike with the mouthpiece open on my helmet. Even though it was a bit uncomfortable they didn't really bother me: it was more funny than anything.

I met a couple hiking in Black Watch kilts; the famous dark green and navy tartan worn by soldiers in the equally famous regiment. They'd had a bet and lost it, so had to complete the walk in their kilts.

The rain started later that day: it was torrential. I stayed in my tent for another night and day. It could have turned into four or five days quite easily: but I knew I must continue on.

I felt that I had relived some of my own heritage and history: that I'd walked the path my ancestors would have walked. And that made me feel surprisingly warm (even though it was wet and cold).

At Edinburgh Castle

Aunty June at Edinburgh Castle

CHAPTER FORTY

No Rain in Spain

INSTEAD of hostelling (or hotelling) in Barcelona, I tried Airbnb.com: the holiday home rental company that gives you options ranging from couch-surfing to luxury accommodation, all in properties that are normally residential homes. The initial philosophy of Airbnb was to enjoy a holiday that was less commercialised, to stay off the beaten track.

I paid $28 a night to stay in a place near Park Güell, one of Antoni Gaudí's inventions. What a view! I could see the entire city and the ocean from my place. Being so close to one of Gaudí's major works was incredible. The Park he'd created in the early 1900s is indicative of his instantly recognisable style. He created imaginatively ornamental buildings that look like something out of a fantasy film set. He's also responsible for La Sagrada Familia: the spired cathedral in central Barcelona which has become a famous landmark. He designed another seventeen buildings in the city including Casa Battlo, a fantastic modernist building of wavy lines, colourful mosaics and an arched roof that looks like the back of a dragon. It's crazy and I loved it!

Transport in Barcelona was excellent: trains and buses that went where I needed to go. Even though the population there isn't that large for a major city (only 1.6 million), nearly eight million tourists visit each year. I guess the infrastructure is built to handle tourists and not just the residents.

In 2015 the first woman was elected into power; a 40 year-old named Ada Colau. She's been called the world's most radical mayor due to her social activism: she considers herself the visible face of the citizens. She cut her mayoral wage by 75% and changed the official car from an Audi to an efficient minivan. Barcelona really is an example of the democratic-socialist revolution taking place in some parts of Europe.

I found a Spanish acupuncturist who said he had a Mexican wife because they were easier to manage than Spanish. He continued, "Blow Spanish women, they're demanding and spoilt and don't do what they're told, unlike Mexican women."

There was one really frightening incident in Barcelona. I got a taxi one day and the driver was creepy. He kept making inappropriate comments about my body and kept trying to touch my leg. I had a feeling that he had bad plans on his mind. I turned around and told him that if he dared try anything I would kill him. After that he kicked me out of the cab in a less than desirable part of Barcelona. He just left me there! Luckily I made my way safely back into the city though, thank God.

I met so many interesting people while I was in Barcelona. I met a Jewish couple called Alexi (Spanish) and Sophia (Russian). They told me how they had to leave Russia because of human rights issues under Putin. They not only showed me around Barcelona and gave me free passes to the museums but also introduced me to a few friends of theirs. One even offered me his apartment in St Petersburg, so I have to go back!

They also told me a lot about what it's like to live in Spain; from the nationwide mortgage crisis where four hundred thousand homes were foreclosed to what happens to bankrupts here. Unlike the United States of America where debts are cleared in their entirety, in Spain you must pay back every cent you owe. Until you die.

Like Queenstown, the high level of tourism into Barcelona has inflated the house prices, so the price of accommodation in Barcelona has become a very real concern.

PAMPLONA

Pamplona is famous for its annual Running of the Bulls: San Fermin the annual festival that involves running through the streets in front of loose cattle. The tradition started randomly in the early fourteenth century because farmers were trying to hurry their cattle along so they could get to the market quicker. They'd scare and excite the bulls into charging and eventually it turned into a race, with the farmers running ahead of the bulls and trying to stay out of harm's way. Every year a series of fences are erected to guide the bulls through the city and provide safety for spectators. Around one hundred people are injured annually but very few of them are from being gored (although 15 people have been killed by bulls since 1910). The day before the festival opens is the Running of the Nudes — where animal protesters run in their underwear and fake bull horns through the streets.

Pamplona for me was not about animal madness; it was more about exploring the city. And what a glorious city it is!

I can imagine in July it would be overrun with tourists here to see the bulls (the city triples and sometimes even quadruples in size); when I was there it was the end of summer, much quieter yet still warm. But the overwhelming memory of Pamplona was the food. Oh, the FOOD. Garroticos (miniature chocolate croissants), piquillo (peppers stuffed with cod), beautiful beans cooked with spices and herbs I couldn't even begin to describe, lots of salmon and trout (filled with cured ham) and pintxos (tapas) on every corner. My mouth is watering just thinking about it...

Again I used Airbnb, but this time it wasn't quite as successful. My flatmate for the night had a mini marijuana plantation in the lounge.

From Pamplona I took the train to Lourdes in France. It's just a quick hop over the border!

LOURDES, FRANCE

Lourdes is a pilgrim hot spot in France; it's the third most important Catholic pilgrim site to visit after Rome and the Holy Land.

The story goes that in 1858 a young girl saw apparitions of the Virgin Mary in a grotto. Since then pilgrims visit the spring in the grotto, which is said to have magical healing powers, and thousands of miracles have been reported from there. Apparently in 1857, the year before the apparition, it was a modest town of only four thousand people. Even today it only has about fifteen thousand people. Only a small town at the bottom of the Pyrenees, Lourdes has to cater to around six million tourists a year because of important religious areas here. But it has a lot of hotels.

I loved this story and while I was there I got to see gatherings of outdoor prayer by candlelight, thousands of them! It was really quite beautiful.

But Google mapping is a bit suspect here; what was supposed to be a 10-minute walk to a local village took me an hour!

CHAPTER FORTY-ONE

The Maverick Pilgrim

L EGEND has it that the walk through north western Spain passes over the remains of St James the Great, one of the twelve apostles. So, it has attracted hundreds of thousands of pilgrims over the years.

I do truly believe the best part of travelling is meeting people, locals or other tourists for that matter.

This got me thinking that walking part of the St James Way would let me mingle with the locals, and I was sure I would meet a range of interesting people. I mean you've got to be interesting if you're crazy enough to walk over hundreds, sometimes thousands, of miles on an ancient pilgrimage, right?

I find some people were fundamentalist about the pilgrim trail and needed to do the whole thing start to finish and clock up thousands of

The Pilgrim Passport

kilometres to feel justified in doing it. Not me though, I was happy to do it part way and bit by bit; I knew before I started that I wasn't going to be able to do the whole walk at once.

We always find reasons not to do things, to travel, to walk, to hike and to go on pilgrimages.

The route I chose was the Camino del Norte or the Northern Way, which officially starts at San Sebastián near the French border and wends westward along the Spanish coast of the Bay of Biscay, and eventually inland toward the Cathedral at Santiago de Compostela. I started out from the coastal French border town of Hendaye, south of Bayonne and just across

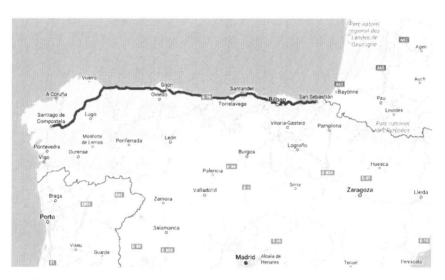

El Camino Del Norte, the Northern Way, is the heavy dark line from San Sebastián in the east to Santiago de Compostela in the west, the usual direction of travel. This map was drawn for the present book, using Google Maps as a base. The French border town of Hendaye from which I set out is not shown in this map.
Map data © 2016 Google and Inst. Geogr. Nacional *(Spain)*

the border from Irun.

In this section, I talk about arriving in San Sebastián after a short walk from Hendaye, less than twenty kilometres. But that was just the first stage of a longer journey, the Camino proper, which I cover in my book *A Maverick Pilgrim Way.*

Most of the Northern Way consists of well-paved concrete surfaces, which ironically enough makes it harder than natural, irregular ground. Long walks along hard and even pavements jar your feet and legs and can give you shin splints. I found the Northern Way harder than walking in the Canadian Rockies and the Himalayas to be honest. It was extremely difficult. But the stunning coastline was blissful; I had nothing but the view to think about (once I tuned out the discomfort in my feet).

I met a Dutch woman, Maron, who ran an organic shop in the north of Holland. We clicked instantly; we laughed, joked around and decided to do the journey together. We walked to San Sebastián, past hundreds of fat and juicy organic animals.

Many places along this walk are beautiful: but seriously, San Sebastián is amazing! The cobblestoned old town contrasted with world-class restaurants overlooking the golden sands and turquoise waters of the Bay of Biscay.

This place was bursting with fashion and film events and the huge villas looking onto the coast were thoughtfully built to blend in with the environment. The modern architecture was exciting and innovative and brilliantly juxtaposed with the dozens of centuries-old churches. It was gorgeous; I fell in love with it.

While we were staying in San Sebastián I met a woman who was half Basque and half Spanish. She told me that because she wasn't *full* Basque she was discriminated against.

She said that the government was trying to take her house off her and public transport cost her more. I suggested she put her property on Airbnb to make a little extra income.

The Basque people in Spain are fascinating. They're already autonomous from Spain and have the right of self- determination over health and their education system.

That means the Basque language, famously unrelated to any other, is used throughout their schools.

It was wonderful walking with my friend Maron. People travel, and hike, for different reasons. For me it is all about the people you meet, and the memories you create. We saw some beautiful places in Spain.

I can't give too much away here but for my complete story on the trails, routes and ways I have done all over Europe it's all in my book *A Maverick Pilgrim Way*, which will also contain many more photographs of the beautiful sights I saw in Russia.

Peterhof, St Petersburg, Russia

In love with Gaudí, Barcelona

Top of Mont Blanc with Jean-Claude

Camden Markets

Epilogue

I haven't worked in a traditional environment since I was a teacher two decades ago, because of my savvy property investments.

I never planned on being a landlord and, even now that I'm a successful one, I still hate it. As a "job" it lacks creativity; it's something I accidentally fell into. But I can't deny that it's given me the freedom to pursue my main passion in life: travel.

I couldn't imagine having any other "career" — nothing else would give me the physical and financial freedom to do what I want, when I want.

And now, I'm able to sit down and write books about all the incredible adventures I have had, I feel blessed.

Not just because I have been able to travel widely, but also because I have been given a chance to give something back. For what is the use of finding out knowledge, if you do not pass it on?

Thanks To

I would like to thank my editor, Chris Harris.

I would also like to thank Liz Keizerwaard.

I would like to sincerely thank my friends
- you know who you are.

And my father Brian Walker, who helped with the book.

And lastly I'd like to thank all of the people
I've met along the way.

Any mistakes, omissions or errors that
remain are, of course, all mine.

Made in the USA
San Bernardino, CA
01 October 2017